Günter Eich
Pigeons and Moles

Günter Eich
Photograph by Hilde Zemann, Munich

Pigeons and Moles

Selected Writings
of
GÜNTER EICH

Translated with an
Introduction
by

Michael Hamburger

CAMDEN HOUSE

Simultaneously published as
volume 62 in
Studies in German Literature, Linguistics, and Culture
Co-published with Skoob Books, Ltd., London.
Authorized American edition by arrangement with
Suhrkamp Verlag
German text © Suhrkamp Verlag 1990
Translations and introductory material:
Copyright © Michael Hamburger 1990
Photograph of Eich © Hilde Zemann
Published by Camden House, Inc.
Drawer 2025
Columbia, SC 29202 USA

Printed on acid-free paper.
Binding materials are chosen for strength and
durability.

ISBN: 0-938100-96-3

Library of Congress Cataloging-in-Publication Data

Eich, Günter, 1907-1972.
 [Selections. English. 1991]
 Pigeons and moles : selected writings of Günter Eich / translated
with an introduction by Michael Hamburger.
       p.   cm. -- (Studies in German literature, linguistics, and
culture : v. 62)
 Translations of selected radio plays and poems.
 Includes bibliographical references.
 ISBN: 0-938100-96-3
 1. Eich, Günter, 1907-1972--Translations, English. I. Hamburger,
Michael. II. Title. III. Series.
PT2609.I17A24 1991   91-8251
                                                              CIP

CONTENTS

These translations are dedicated to
Christopher Holme, who produced the radio plays,
and to Anne Beresford, who acted in some of them.

Biographical Note

GÜNTER EICH WAS BORN in 1907 at Lebus on the Oder, Mecklenburg. After studying Economics and Chinese in Berlin and Paris, he became a full-time writer as early as 1932, having published early poems under a pseudonym in 1927 and a first book of poems in 1930. Thematically, the early poems were close to the 'nature poetry' of Oskar Loerke and Wilhelm Lehmann, formally they showed the influence of Gottfried Benn. Among his coevals, Eich's closest affinity was to Peter Huchel, to whom he remained devoted in later years. From 1933 to 1945, the duration of the Third Reich, he published only in periodicals, also working for the radio before his conscription. After war service as a soldier and his release in 1946 from an American prisoner-of-war camp, he re-emerged as an author. From 1950 onwards he earned his living mainly as a writer of radio plays, producing as many as four of them in some years. His first post-war collection of poems, *Abgelegene Gehöfte*, appeared in 1948, followed by *Untergrundbahn* in 1949 and *Botschaften des Regens* in 1955.

In 1953 Günter Eich married the writer Ilse Aichinger. Their children are Clemens, also a poet, and Miriam. The family lived mainly in the border region between Bavaria and Austria, but Eich travelled widely in the years up to his death in 1972.

His principal collections of radio plays were *Träume* (1953), *Stimmen* (1958) and *In Anderen Sprachen* (1964).

It was with the publication of his book of poems *Zu den Akten* in 1964 that controversies about his later manner began. The gap of nine years between this collection and the preceding one may have made the change conspicuous. Two more collections of poems followed in 1966 and 1972. The prose poems which Eich called 'moles' began to appear in 1967 and were gathered into one volume in 1972.

The four-volume *Gesammelte Werke* edition was published in 1973 by Suhrkamp, Frankfurt.

INTRODUCTION

GÜNTER EICH WAS ONE of the first outstandingly good poets to emerge from what an older survivor, Wilhelm Lehmann, called 'the second Flood' — from the 'inner emigration' of honest writers under the Third Reich and from the spate of well-meaning but largely mediocre verse released for publication by its collapse. Although he had established a small reputation before 1933, it was based on juvenile work. By 1945 he was a mature writer, old enough not to be carried away by the euphoria of liberation, and determined to preserve his independence of mind in all circumstances and conditions, not excluding his term as a prisoner-of-war.

Despite controversies about the relative merit of his earlier and later work, in the German-speaking countries Günter Eich has been accepted as a twentieth-century classic — for what that is worth, at a time when the conditions and canons that made literary classics look like becoming an anachronism, to be replaced by cults of personality, on the one hand, by quantitative computations of sales on the other. Not long before his death Eich said in an interview: 'Perhaps very soon Eich will be passé ... How I'm regarded after that makes no difference to me.' Publicly, if not in his heart, Eich had recognized the age of post-literacy. Within a year of his death in 1972, his complete works — running to some two thousand pages — were collected and published; and that four-volume edition is due to be superseded by a second one, emended and enlarged.

In Britain, though, Eich's work received little critical attention outside the universities even at the period when five of his radio plays were produced on what was the Third Programme of the BBC and two of them were available in book form. Unlike quite a number of German authors whose reputations in their own language area are less secure than his, Eich seems not to have penetrated into any sort of general awareness in the Englishspeaking world.

One reason for that may be that in Britain and America — with a few exceptions — radio plays never attained the prominence *as literature* which they attained in Germany in the 1950s and 1960s, before the hegemony of television; and, although at that period almost all the best German writers wrote radio plays, Günter Eich was acknowledged to be the supreme master of that medium, which he had taken up even before the war, when the radio play had not begun to be taken seriously as an art form. Eich's post-war radio plays were widely read, as well as listened to, and studied in schools and universities, like his poems.

As a poet, Eich became one of the initiators of a distinctly post-war phase in German literature with his collection of 1948, containing the poems he had written in an American prisoner-of-war camp, represented here by 'Inventory' and 'Latrine.' (That 'Inventory' parodies a pre-war poem by a Czech writer available in a German version, does not detract from the singularity of Eich's poem. Its matter and its tone were entirely his own.) Other poems in that collection went back to Eich's pre-war work as a so-called nature poet; and it was the clash of the two modes not only within a single collection but within the poems themselves to which 'Inventory' and 'Latrine' owed their shock effect.

Over the next few years the poems of his with the most immediate impact were those from the book version of his radio play *Träume* (Dreams) — poems more rhetorical and hortatory than any included in his books of poems of any period:

THINK OF THIS, THAT MAN IS THE ENEMY OF MAN,
And that he schemes destruction.
Think of this always, think of this now
At one moment in April,
Under this clouded sky,
While you think you are hearing growth as a gentle rustling
And girl labourers hoe thistles
Under the skylark's song;
At this moment, too, think of it ...

Think of this when a hand touches you tenderly,
Think of this in your wife's embrace.
Think of this when your child laughs.

Think of this, that after the great destructions
Everyone will prove that he was innocent.

Think of this:
Nowhere on the map do Korea and Bikini lie
But in your own heart.

Pigeons and Moles

Think of this, that you are guilty of every horror
Enacted far from you —
...

Another of these poems was

WAKE UP, FOR YOUR DREAMS ARE BAD!
Keep awake, because the horror draws nearer.

It will come to you also who live far away from the
        places where blood is shed,
to you also and to your afternoon nap
from which you don't like to be roused.
If it won't come today it will come tomorrow,
but be sure it will come ...

...

No, don't sleep while those manage the world are busy!
Mistrust their power, which they claim they need to
        assume for your sake!
See to it, wakeful, that your hearts are not empty when
they count on the emptiness of your hearts!
Do what is useless, sing the songs that no one expects
        you to sing!
Be awkward, be sand, not oil, in the works of the world!

As Peter Horst Neumann has shown in his perceptive short study (1981), the anarchism imputed to Eich's later work did not represent anything like as sharp a break with his earlier stances as the reviewers made out. Even Eich's early 'nature poems' were full of doubt and unease about the human condition; and this 'nature poetry' had flourished in Germany among the 'inner emigration' during the Third Reich as a form of resistance not punishable by internment or death. (Gottfried Benn had described military service as another form of such emigration — an 'aristocratic' one!). Up to *Botschaften des Regens*, true, nature had offered Eich an alternative to the human condition — hints and messages of a truth or reality of which non-human nature was the repository. A similar magic had informed the poems of Loerke and Lehmann, though hardly the poems of Gottfried Benn, the Nietzschean hankerer after regressions into pre-civilized, pre-animal, pre-vegetable unconsciousness, and professed nihilist. The outstanding poems in Eich's collection of 1948, the camp poems, owed their power to the stark collision of the realities of a debased form of human existence with the by now dubious and fleeting comforts which generations of Romantic and Symbolist poets had sought in the natural world. In his next collection, *Untergrundbahn* — whose very title prefigured the underground proclivities of Eich's moles — Eich was still less a 'nature poet' in any accepted sense of the word, turning his attention to every-day life in the cities. As for the anarchism, even the hortatory poems from which I have quoted here are not manifestoes of any of the going political positivisms, but deeply subversive and sceptical of them all. The commitment in them is an ethical and religious, not a political one.

Nor were the messages received by Eich when he was writing the contents of his most mature collection of what he was still prepared to designate as 'nature poems,' *Botschaften des Regens*, the comforting ones received by most of his predecessors. They are hints of general destruction, and of human responsibility for that destruction; 'messages of despair,' 'messages of poverty,' 'messages of reproach' in the title poem of the collection. The consciousness that pervades them is a post-nuclear one. The only faith that Eich shared with his immediate predecessors and with earlier ones — the Romantic writers Novalis, Jean Paul and Eichendorff — is that in the cryptic meaningfulness of messages conveyed by the natural world. Yet the poem 'Fragment' from the same collection not only casts doubt on his ability ever to discover the one, 'unique' word that would unlock the mystery, but anticipates his abandonment of this magical, if not mystical, quest. The comfort in 'End of a Summer' is that trees are as mortal and mutable as we are, that the 'bird script' of migrating flocks corresponds to premonitions of human death. It is the correspondence alone — Baudelaire's 'forest of symbols' — that gave Eich a tenuous foothold in the Romantic-Symbolist tradition; the correspondence alone, not the gist of the messages received, to which, for a while, he could resort for comfort.

What was positive in all of Eich's writings up to his later radio plays was the search for an alternative order to that which had collapsed in 1945, leaving a vacuum known as 'zero point' and the determination that even writers not overtly political would never again give so much as passive support to a regime like the one Eich had served as a soldier. Because the disillusionment was so widely shared — at the period when German writers formed themselves into the *Gruppe 47* — the charge of anarchism was not raised against Eich's questioning of all political power in poems, radio plays and in his Darmstadt speech. The charge was raised when a new political positivism, largely neo-Marxist, had come to dominate the West German media. The change of stance and tone in Eich's work — and there was such a change — may have a great deal to do with his refusal to embrace that new positivism. (Anarchism and Marxism had been at loggerheads ever since Marx's lifetime. It was an anarchist socialist, Gustav Landauer, who wrote a prophetic indictment of Marxist materialism before the Russian Revolution — from a point of view implicitly religious; and Günter Eich admitted that his search for an alternative order had been an implicitly religious one.)

The radio plays, too, are imaginative explorations of realities and correspondences not given but sought. Eich put it this way, in a comment written in 1956:

'My existence is an attempt of this kind, to accept reality unseen. Writing, too, is possible on that basis. But I also try to write something that tends elsewhere. I mean poems.

I write poems so as to orientate myself in reality. I regard them as trigometric points or as buoys that mark my course across an unknown plane.

Only through writing do things attain reality for me. Reality is not my premise but my aim. I have to produce reality.'

He went on to describe all writing as an act of translation. 'We translate without having the original text. The most successful translation comes closest to that original text and attains the highest degree of reality.'

Introduction

The magical paradox is even more pointedly formulated at the end of Eich's radio play of 1957, *Allah has a Hundred Names*: 'One has to translate, if the original is beyond one's comprehension.'

True, in the 'mole' or prose poems 'Housemates,' Eich did pronounce a related curse both on 'Father State' and 'Mother Nature.' If we consider the ancestry of those concepts, and the war fought out between them in European cultures ever since Rousseau, if not long before him, it becomes impossible to posit any basis for Eich's later stance compatible even with anarchism, because anarchism rests on the assumption or hope that at some point in time human beings will be adult enough to liberate themselves from the tutelage of 'Father State' and become fit to govern themselves. This assumption or hope has always come out on the side of 'Mother Nature' — against 'Father State.' If Günter Eich's curse on both is to be taken seriously at all, his later stance becomes a mystical one; and again it is Far Eastern modes of thought that constitute a precedent for the jocularity and playfulness of its mysticism. Zen Buddhism is one precedent that springs to mind: ritualized mockeries and provocations, absurdities that serve to jerk the initiate out of rational constrictions, towards a higher order of perception. That Eich should leave such mystical implications implicit in his sardonic word games is quite consistent with his earlier practices as a writer; and so is the mysticism itself.

Because the radio play renders no reality that is seen, it was the best of all possible media for the more elaborate of Eich's magical searches and evocations. More often than not the diction of his radio plays is that of realistic, colloquial dialogue; but their meaning lies in their mysterious juxtapositions, correspondences and parallels — as in the interweaving of at least two plots, the Third Reich German and the post-war Italian, in *The Girls from Viterbo*, with the persecution of Christians in Roman times as a third, recondite, sub-plot and pointer to the others. Realistic plausibility did not inhibit Eich's inventions in his radio plays. As in fable and fairy tale, human characters were interchangeable with non-human ones — a tiger in *Der Tiger Jussuf*, a bird in *Sabeth*. As for *The Year Lacertis*, in it the search for reality and meaning become partly lexical — as in the Allah play also — with the most various changes rung on the magical key word 'Lacertis' itself and its etymological or semantic potentialities. One such magical key is the German idiom 'dran glauben müssen,' which Eich used as the epigraph to *The Rolling Sea at Setúbal*.

xv

Equating certainty with death, impossible to render in English, it is subliminally present throughout *The Year Lacertis*.

The first version of *The Year Lacertis* was written as early as 1953, more than a decade before Eich withdrew from the publicly exemplary functions expected of prominent writers in Germany — an expectation to which he could still respond with exemplary trenchancy in his Darmstadt speech of 1959, however anarchically.

I have indicated one factor in Eich's withdrawal from that function — a social and political factor, to do with the ideological demands made on West German writers in the late 'sixties and early 'seventies, demands that threatened the imaginative freedom in which all of Eich's work had its being. Another extraneous factor was the decline of the radio play into a minority medium at the same period, when Eich experimented with puppet plays, but could not or would not adapt to the requirements of conventional television drama. A more deep-seated reason for the sardonic playfulness of Eich's later work — so offensive to many of his readers, because it seemed not only anarchic, but nihilistic or solipsistic — was the loss of his faith in nature as a repository of arcane truths. Baudelaire, among others, had called nature a 'dictionary' — meaning that it is a repository of symbols. More and more, Eich drew not on that dictionary, but on actual dictionaries, encyclopedias, atlases, and arbitrary concatenations of their contents for his inventions. It was a desperate resort; but the nonsense of the later poems and prose poems was not only Eich's alternative to total silence, but a defiant enactment of the freedom denied to writers by the dominant ideologists. This nonsense of his contains a good deal of sense — much of it very bitter — and a good deal of criticism, social and otherwise, that goes deeper than the social criticism in fashion at the time. True to his anarchic commitment, if not to his earlier magical quest, Eich continued to shock, perplex and irritate his readers, to be 'sand, not oil, in the works of the world.'

In 'Footnote to Rome,' for instance, the absence of Japanese miniature gardens becomes an indictment of all 'the grandeur that was Rome'; and this casual indictment is supported by the minimalism and miniaturism of all Eich's later texts — those of a writer who had begun as a student of Chinese and produced a substantial collection of translations of Chinese poems in the years between 1949 and 1951. If Eich's critique of political power in all his phases rested less on

Romantic affinities than on Far Eastern, especially Taoist ones — and this strikes me as quite conceivable — the reduction he practiced in his later work constitutes not a break in his development but a culmination, as far as his art is concerned.

The increasingly lexical procedures of Eich's later inventions must also have something to do with his specialization as a radio dramatist over a long period, going back to his beginnings as a writer. Between 1932 and 1972 Eich wrote at least forty-six radio plays, not counting the variant versions of some of them. Considering that the radio play is an aural medium, made of words, just as poems are, supported only by sound effects, without the constraints imposed by visible characters, their actions and settings, it is not so very astonishing that words tended to become the characters of Eich's later poems and prose, including his last radio plays. In poems and prose poems, admittedly, these characters could be seen, as well as heard, becoming ideograms or cryptograms in the process — to be 'meditated,' Eich said, rather than interpreted; in which case the magic, too, entered into his later work by the back door, under the guise of nonsense or sheer fun.

What few of his readers will swallow — and the pervasive absurdism of the texts absolves them from swallowing — is Eich's own claim, in an interview of 1971, that he was now 'committed against the establishment — not only in society, but in the whole of creation.' Asked about the reason for the 'total change' in his manner and attitudes, Eich replied: 'Much of that has religious grounds. In my book of poems Messages of the Rain I was still a nature poet, who accepted creation. Today I no longer accept nature, even if it is unalterable. I am against agreement with the things in creation. It's always the same train of thought: a "no-longer-being-in-agreement".' The extreme brevity of that interview and its pugnacious tone throughout suggests that if Eich's tongue was not in his cheek, his eyes were on the door handle.

One blaring instance of the provocative perversity of Eich's later stance is his title 'Long Poems' for the very shortest, haiku-like, verses in the sequence of that name. This must have been his response to the controversy about long poems, as advocated by Walter Höllerer, current at the time in West German periodicals.

A more reliable characterization of his later poems dates from 1968:

... So, armed with scepticism, I will list some points of my poetics, a private list of desiderata, nothing more. This and thus I should like to write:
    Poems without the dimension of time
    Poems that have to be meditated, not interpreted
    Poems that are beautiful without containing beauty
    Poems in which one simultaneously expresses and conceals
     oneself
    Unwise poems
    Direct poems

... Lyrical poetry is superfluous, useless, ineffectual. This is what legitimizes it in a utilitarian world. Lyrical poetry does not speak the language of power — this is its hidden explosive charge.

Here the word 'ineffectual' echoes a well-known statement by Gottfried Benn on the same subject; but Eich's anarchism was still distinct from the nihilism that Benn professed both before and after the war, revoking it only in a late note not written for publication. Even at this late stage Eich maintained his opposition to power; and the very ineffectualness of poetry, which was his justification for the playful freedom of his later writings, is qualified, if not contradicted, by what he says about its 'hidden explosive charge.' 'Hidden' is the key word to all of Eich's poetic procedures, early and late. Pigeons and other birds fascinated him with the elusiveness of flight and height. The German word for mole, 'Maulwurf,' denotes a creature that throws up (soil) with its mouth or maw. The mole is hidden, subterranean, subversive, an irritation to gardeners, because it undermines their order of lawns and flowerbeds, but useful to them, too, as a destroyer of noxious grubs.

POEMS 1945~1955

INVENTUR

Dies ist meine Mütze,
dies ist mein Mantel,
hier mein Rasierzeug
im Beutel aus Leinen.

Konservenbüchse:
Mein Teller, mein Becher,
ich hab in das Weißblech
den Namen geritzt.

Geritzt hier mit diesem
kostbaren Nagel,
den vor begehrlichen
Augen ich berge.

Im Brotbeutel sind
ein Paar wollene Socken
und einiges, was ich
niemand verrate,

so dient es als Kissen
nachts meinem Kopf.
Die Pappe hier liegt
zwischen mir und der Erde.

Die Bleistiftmine
lieb ich am meisten:
Tags schreibt sie mir Verse,
die nachts ich erdacht.

Dies ist mein Notizbuch,
dies meine Zeltbahn,
dies ist mein Handtuch,
dies ist mein Zwirn.

INVENTORY

This is my cap,
this is my greatcoat,
and here's my shaving kit
in its linen bag.

A can of meat:
my plate, my mug,
into its tin
I've scratched my name.

Scratched it with this
invaluable nail
which I keep hidden
from covetous eyes.

My bread bag holds
two woollen socks
and a couple of things
I show to no one,

like that it serves me
as a pillow at night.
Between me and the earth
I lay this cardboard.

This pencil lead
is what I love most:
by day it writes verses
I thought up in the night.

This is my notebook
and this is my groundsheet,
this is my towel,
this is my thread.

LATRINE

Über stinkendem Graben,
Papier voll Blut and Urin,
umschwirrt von funkelnden Fliegen,
hocke ich in den Knien,

den Blick auf bewaldete Ufer,
Gärten, gestrandetes Boot.
In den Schlamm der Verwesung
klatscht der versteinte Kot.

Irr mir im Ohre schallen
Verse von Hölderlin.
In schneeiger Reinheit spiegeln
Wolken sich im Urin.

'Geh aber nun und grüße
die schöne Garonne — '
Unter den schwankenden Füßen
schwimmen die Wolken davon.

LATRINE

Over the stinking drain ditch,
paper all bloody, bepissed,
with glittering flies around it,
crouching, I strain and twist,

my gaze on riverbanks, wooded,
gardens, a boat pulled up.
Into the mire of corruption
petrified faeces plop.

Mad in my hearing echo
verses by Holderlin.
In snowy pureness, mirrored,
clouds in the urine are seen.

'But go now with a greeting
to the beautiful Garonne —'
Under my tottering feet those
cloudlets have drifted, are gone.

DER NACHMITTAG

Der Nachmittag rührt dich an
mit seiner unsichtbaren, gewichtlosen, schrecklichen Hand.
Auf den Dachziegeln wächst in grünen Flecken das Moos.
Was bewegt sich? Ein Sperling fliegt auf. Ein Rauch, der sich kräuselt.

Noch einen schmerzhaften, innigen Augenblick,
dann werden die Bilder hinschmelzen. Die Quecksilbersäule
schnellt hinauf und fällt in lautlos rasendem Wechsel.
Die Aggregatzustände verändern sich.
Häuser werden zu Flüssigem und der Rauch zu Stein.

Oh unbarmherzige Stille, die in den Ohren rauscht!
Die Welt hebt sich auf in der endlich gefundenen Gleichung.
Auch dein Herzschlag ward nicht verworfen. Oh sei getrost,
eben half er zum Untergang.

THE AFTERNOON

The afternoon touches you
with its invisible, weightless, terrible hand.
On the rooftiles moss grows in pads of green.
What is moving? A sparrow flies up. A column of smoke frays.

One more painful and poignant moment,
then the things you see will melt down. The quicksilver thread
shoots up and falls in noiselessly frenzied fits.
The aggregate states are changing.
Houses liquify, the smoke turns to stone.

Oh, merciless silence that roars in our ears!
The world dissolves in the long-sought equation.
Nor was your heartbeat rejected. Never doubt or fear
that just now it helped towards annihilation.

FRAGMENT

Das Wort, das einzige! Immer suche ichs,
das wie Sesam die Türen der Berge öffnet,
es, durch die gläsern gewordenen Dinge blickend
ins Unsichtbare —

Wörter waren vergebens. Oh Vokabeln der Seele, Versuch,
ohnmächtiger, zu benennen den Flug der Taube, da schon
                                       gewiß ward,
daß die Rose sich färbt unter anderem Zwange, in solcher
Beugung sich nicht die Berge beugten.
Noch Stummheit immer, Qual des Schluchzens, die dauert.
Schrecklich gepreßt, wie in Erstickens Angst,
mit Augen hervorquellend, so lallt es,
Sprache des Maulwurfs, der Elster Gekrächz.
Du Wort, einziges, allen Wörtern unähnlich und gemeinsam,
ich vernehme dich in den Farben, horche auf dich im Anblick
                                       des Laubs,
wie liegst du mir auf der Zunge!
Du, das ich gekannt habe,
du, dessen ich teilhaft war,
du, das im Schallen des Ohrs ganz nahe ist, —
dennoch faß ich dich
niemals, niemals, niemals!

Du, das Wort, das im Anfang war,
du, so gewiß wie Gott und so unhörbar,
wie soll ich hinnehmen deinen grausamen
Widerspruch, daß unaussprechlich zu sein,
dein Wesen ist, oh Wort — ?

FRAGMENT

The word, the unique one! Always I look for it,
that which like Sesame opens the doors of the mountains,
which peers through the things grown glassy
into what cannot be seen —

Words were in vain. Oh, vocables of the soul, attempt,
ineffectual, to give a name to the pigeon's flight, when it was clear
that under a different compulsion the rose assumes its colour,
not in such declension the mountains bowed.
Still silence always, torment of sobbing that lasts.
Horribly pressed, as in fear of asphyxiation,
with eyeballs bulging, it babbles
mole's language, magpie's cawing.

You word, unique one, unlike all words and common to all,
I hear you in colours, listen to you in looking at leaves,
always there, on the tip of my tongue!
You I have known,
you I have shared in,
you quite near in the tympanum of my ear, —
yet never shall I grasp you,
not ever, ever, ever!

You the word that was in the beginning,
you as certain as God and as inaudible,
how shall I accept your cruel
contradiction, that to be unutterable
is your nature, word — ?

ENDE EINES SOMMERS

Wer möchte leben ohne den Trost der Bäume!

Wie gut, daß sie am Sterben teilhaben!
Die Pfirsiche sind geerntet, die Pflaumen färben sich,
während unter dem Brückenbogen die Zeit rauscht.

Dem Vogelzug vertraue ich meine Verzweiflung an.
Er mißt seinen Teil von Ewigkeit gelassen ab.
Seine Strecken
werden sichtbar im Blattwerk als dunkler Zwang,
die Bewegung der Flügel färbt die Früchte.

Es heißt Geduld haben.
Bald wird die Vogelschrift entsiegelt,
unter der Zunge ist der Pfennig zu schmecken.

END OF A SUMMER

Who would wish to live without the comfort of trees!

What a good thing that they take part in dying!
The peaches have been picked, the plums grow darker
while under the bridge's arch time roars.

To the migrating flock I entrust my despair.
Calmly it measures out its share in eternity.
Its courses
become visible in leafage as dark compulsion,
the motion of wings colours the fruit.

What's needed is patience.
Soon the bird script will be unsealed,
the penny under my tongue begins to taste.

BOTSCHAFTEN DES REGENS

Nachrichten, die für mich bestimmt sind,
weitergetrommelt von Regen zu Regen,
von Schiefer- zu Ziegeldach,
eingeschleppt wie eine Krankheit,
Schmuggelgut, dem überbracht,
der es nicht haben will —

Jenseits der Wand schallt das Fensterblech,
rasselnde Buchstaben, die sich zusammenfügen,
und der Regen redet
in der Sprache, von welcher ich glaubte,
niemand kenne sie außer mir —

Bestürzt vernehme ich
die Botschaften der Verzweiflung,
die Botschaften der Armut
und die Botschaften des Vorwurfs.
Es kränkt mich, daß sie an mich gerichtet sind,
denn ich fühle mich ohne Schuld.

Ich spreche es laut aus,
daß ich den Regen nicht fürchte und seine Anklagen
und den nicht, der sie mir zuschickte,
daß ich zu guter Stunde
hinausgehen und ihm antworten will.

MESSAGES OF THE RAIN

News intended for me,
drummed out from rain to rain,
from slate roof to tiled roof,
introduced like an illness,
contraband, delivered to him
who has no wish to receive it.

Beyond the wall my metal window-sill clamors,
pattering letters link up
and the rain speaks
in that language which once I believed
none but I could decipher —

Disconcerted now I hear
the messages of despair,
the messages of poverty
and the messages of reproach.
It hurts me to think they're addressed to me,
feeling guiltless of any offence.

And I say out loud
that I do not fear the rain or its accusations,
nor him who sent them to me;
and that all in good time
I will go out and give him my answer.

STRANDGUT

Bruchstücke von Gesprächen,
die unter Wasser geführt werden,
auf den Sand geworfene Antworten, —

Keine Fährten, aber die Wellenränder
mit Quallen and Algenteilchen,
Holzsplitter, Muschelschale und Bernsteinrest,
und die Welle, die zurückläuft,
daß hinter der Feuchtigkeit
der Sand sich wieder erhellt,
als begebe sich eine schnelle Dämmerung.

Die Frage erwartend
flattert das Gras auf der Düne.

JETSAM

Fragments of conversations
that take place under water,
answers thrown on the sand, —

No wakes but the tips of waves
with jellyfish and particles of seaweed,
wood splinters, empty sea-shell and amber remains
and the wave that runs back
so that behind the wetness
the sand brightens again
as though with a sudden dawn.

Awaiting the question
the dune grasses flutter.

STRAND MIT QUALLEN

Sterntaler, Meertaler,
geprägt in der Schmiede des Wassers
unter der Herrschaft nicht mehr verehrter Könige.
Silberner Schleim, erstarrt im Dezemberfrost.
Undeutbar
das rötlich durchscheinende Wappentier,
hieroglyphisch die Inschrift.

Verborgen sind die Märkte,
wo Tangwälder von Träumen gehandelt werden,
Anteile am Regen, der ins Meer fällt,
und das Bürgerrecht versunkener Städte.

Die Armut bückt sich nicht,
die Kiefer dreht sich landeinwärts.
Niemand wird erwartet außer dem Wind.

BEACH WITH JELLYFISH

Star dollar, sand dollar,
minted in the water's forge
under the reign of kings no longer revered.
Silver shine, grown rigid in December frost.
Undecipherable
the redly translucent heraldic beast,
the inscription hieroglyphic.

Hidden are the markets
where seaweed forests of dreams are traded,
shares in the rain that falls into the sea
and the civic rights of cities submerged.

Poverty does not bow,
the pine tree turns inland.
No one's expected, only the wind.

WO ICH WOHNE

Als ich das Fenster öffnete,
schwammen Fische ins Zimmer,
Heringe. Es schien
eben ein Schwarm vorüberzuziehen.
Auch zwischen den Birnbäumen spielten sie.
Die meisten aber
hielten sich noch im Wald,
über den Schonungen und den Kiesgruben.

Sie sind lästig. Lästiger aber sind noch
die Matrosen
(auch höhere Ränge, Steuerleute, Kapitäne),
die vielfach ans offene Fenster kommen
und um Feuer bitten für ihren schlechten Tabak.

Ich will ausziehen.

WHERE I LIVE

When I opened the window
fishes swam into the room,
herrings. A shoal
seemed to be passing.
Between the pear trees too they played.
But most of them
still kept to the forest,
above the sapling plantations and gravel pits.

They're a nuisance. But more of a nuisance
are the sailors
(higher ranks, too, helmsmen, captains)
who keep on coming to the open window
to ask for a light for their cheap tobacco.

I want to move out.

REISE

Du kannst dich abwenden
vor der Klapper des Aussätzigen,
Fenster und Ohren verschließen
und warten, bis er vorbei ist.

Doch wenn du sie einmal gehört hast,
hörst du sie immer,
und weil er nicht weggeht,
mußt du gehen.

Packe ein Bündel zusammen, das nicht zu schwer ist,
denn niemand hilft tragen.
Mach dich verstohlen davon und laß die Tür offen,
du kommst nicht wieder.

Geh weit genug, ihm zu entgehen,
fahre zu Schiff oder suche die Wildnis auf:
Die Klapper des Aussätzigen verstummt nicht.

Du nimmst sie mit, wenn er zurückbleibt.
Horch, wie das Trommelfell klopft
vom eigenen Herzschlag!

JOURNEY

You can turn away
from the leper's rattle,
shut your windows and ears,
wait until he has passed.

But if once you have heard it
you'll hear it always,
and because he won't go
you must go.

Pack up a bundle that's not too heavy,
for no one will help you carry.
Creep away softly and leave the door open,
you will not return.

Go far enough to get away from him,
board a ship or look for a wilderness:
the leper's rattle will not fall silent.

If he stays behind you will take it with you.
That tapping on your eardrums — listen! —
is your own heartbeat.

IN ANDEREN SPRACHEN

Wenn der Elsternflug mich befragte,
das Wippen der Bachstelze,
in allen Jahrhunderten vor meiner Geburt,
wenn das Stumme mich fragte,
gab mein Ohr ihm die Antwort.

Heute erinnert mich
der Blick aus dem Fenster.
Ich denke in die Dämmerung,
wo die Antwort auffliegt,
Federn bewegt,
im Ohr sich die Frage rührt.

Während mein Hauch sich noch müht,
das Ungeschiedne zu nennen,
hat mich das Wiesengrün übersetzt
und die Dämmerung denkt mich.

IN OTHER LANGUAGES

When the magpie's flight questioned me,
the wagtail's flicking,
in all the centuries before my birth,
when silent things questioned me
my ear gave the answer.

What reminds me today
is the view from my window.
I think into the twilight
where the answer flies up,
sets feathers into motion,
the question stirs in my ear.

While my breath still labours
to name the undifferentiated
the meadow's green has translated me
and the twilight thinks me.

JAPANISCHER HOLZSCHNITT

Ein rosa Pferd,
gezäumt und gesattelt, —
für wen?

Wie nah der Reiter auch sei,
er bleibt verborgen.

Komm du für ihn,
tritt in das Bild ein
und ergreif die Zügel!

JAPANESE WOODCUT

A pink horse,
bridled and saddled, —
for whom?

However near the rider may be,
he remains concealed.

Come in his stead, then, you,
enter the picture
and seize the reins!

TAUBEN

Taubenflug über die Äcker hin, —
ein Flügelschlag, der schneller ist als die Schönheit.
Sie holt ihn nicht ein, sondern bleibt mir
als Unbehagen zurück im Herzen.

Als wäre auch Taubengelächter vernehmbar
vor den Schlägen, den grün gestrichenen Zwerghäusern,
und ich beginne nachzudenken,
ob der Flug ihnen wichtig ist,
welchen Rang die Blicke zum Erdboden haben
und wie sie das Aufpicken des Korns einordnen
und das Erkennen des Habichts.

Ich rate mir selbst, mich vor den Tauben zu fürchten.
Du bist nicht ihr Herr, sage ich, wenn du Futter streust,
wenn du Nachrichten an ihre Federn heftest,
wenn du Zierformen züchtest, neue Farben,
neue Schöpfe, Gefieder am Fuß.
Vertrau deiner Macht nicht,
so wirst du auch nicht verwundert sein,
wenn du erfährst, daß du unwichtig bist,

daß neben deinesgleichen heimliche Königreiche bestehen,
Sprachen ohne Laut, die nicht erforscht werden,
Herrschaften ohne Macht und unangreifbar,
daß die Entscheidungen geschehen im Taubenflug.

PIGEONS

Flight of pigeons over the ploughed fields —
a wingbeat more swift than beauty
that cannot catch up with such speed
but remains in my heart as discomfort.

As if the laughter of pigeons too could be heard
in front of the dovecotes, dwarf dwellings painted green,
and I begin to consider
whether flight is important to them,
what rank they accord to the earthward glance
and how they value the pecking of grain,
how the recognition of hawks.

I advise myself to be afraid of pigeons.
You are not their master, I say, when you throw them food,
when you fasten messages to their legs,
when you breed curious variants, new colours,
new crests, or tufts of feathers above the feet.
Put no trust in your power,
then you'll not be astonished
when you discover how little you count,

that beside your kind there are hidden kingdoms,
languages without sounds that cannot be studied,
dominions without power and unassailable;
that decisions are made by the pigeons' flight.

THREE RADIO PLAYS
1952~1957

THE GIRLS FROM VITERBO

VOICES: GOLDSCHMIDT, BOTTARI, GIRALDI, EMILIO, GABRIELE, FRAU WINTER, ANGELICA BOTTARI, ANTONIA, LUZIA, LENA, MARIA, BIANCA.

1

GABRIELE: Wake up! Wake up!

GOLDSCHMIDT: *(waking up)* What is it? Gabriele?

GABRIELE: *(whispering)* Footsteps on the stairs!
(They listen)

GOLDSCHMIDT: It's nothing. Any number of people go up and down these stairs. It's nothing to do with us.

GABRIELE: That's what I thought.

GOLDSCHMIDT: But you woke me up all the same.

GABRIELE: It's better to be awake. Your own words, Grandfather.

GOLDSCHMIDT: Yes, it is better.

GABRIELE: I'm always awake. And yet I ought to sleep — at the tender age of seventeen. Isn't that so?

GOLDSCHMIDT: It's advisable to have a good deal of sleep at your age.

GABRIELE: And at your age, Grandfather?

GOLDSCHMIDT: One needs only a little sleep.

GABRIELE: Oh, these wise saws!

GOLDSCHMIDT: What do you mean?

GABRIELE: All these bits of experience, the rubbish I have to listen to, day after day. I'd like to sweep it all away.

GOLDSCHMIDT: Come now, surely it isn't as bad as that.

GABRIELE: Don't cut potatoes with your knife, and at seventy one doesn't need much sleep. My dear old wiseacre of a grandfather, admit that you love sleeping. Not to say, revel in it.

GOLDSCHMIDT: I was glad you woke me.

GABRIELE: Only because I didn't want to have this fear all alone.

GOLDSCHMIDT: When I opened my eyes I thought for a moment that I was somewhere else.

GABRIELE: You ought to know that striped wall-paper by now.

GOLDSCHMIDT: I didn't know it.

GABRIELE: 365 stripes; I've counted them. An absurd coincidence, don't you think?

GOLDSCHMIDT: Probably.

GABRIELE: Or else?

GOLDSCHMIDT: What else could it be?

GABRIELE: As many stripes as there are days in the year.

GOLDSCHMIDT: I understood you the first time. An absurd coincidence, as you say.

GABRIELE: I don't believe it. That there are 365 days in the year is part of the nonsense you go on telling me, you and Frau Winter. There are 365 stripes in the year.

GOLDSCHMIDT: *(sighing)* Yes, yes, of course, if you wish to think so.

GABRIELE: If only you'd contradict me, Grandfather!

GOLDSCHMIDT: Oh, Gabriele.

GABRIELE: *(aping him)* Oh, Gabriele!

GOLDSCHMIDT: When I awoke —

GABRIELE: You were somewhere else. You said that before. Probably you were in the place where we really are.

GOLDSCHMIDT: Unfortunately this is the place where we really are. Berlin, Prinzregentenstrasse —

GABRIELE: October 1943. All very improbable.

GOLDSCHMIDT: What do you say?

GABRIELE: The address, I mean, the date, the stripes on the wallpaper. I don't believe in them.

GOLDSCHMIDT: Just for a moment I had the same feeling.

GABRIELE: When you woke up. But I never believe it. In this place everything is false. When I look out of the window it seems as though it's raining. You say it's the grey face of the house next door. But is that an explanation?

GOLDSCHMIDT: What do you want me to say?

GABRIELE: A bad dream. Why don't you say it? A man of seventy and his granddaughter who have to go into hiding, spend three years in the flat of a noble-minded landlady, can't go out into the street — old wives' tales, the lot of them, and so badly put together that not a second of it all could be true! Why don't you say it?

GOLDSCHMIDT: Oh, Gabriele.

GABRIELE: *(sobbing)* I can't bear it any longer. *(She pulls herself together)* And when you woke up?

GOLDSCHMIDT: I didn't recognize you. I thought you were a girl called Antonia.

GABRIELE: Antonia?

GOLDSCHMIDT: As for me —

GABRIELE: Couldn't it be that my name is Antonia? That everything is really different, with a different wall-paper and without Frau Winter — a completely different life?

GOLDSCHMIDT: As for me, I was a schoolmaster. I even remember my name: Pietro Bottari.

GABRIELE: Pietro?

GOLDSCHMIDT: Bottari. We were all from Viterbo.

GABRIELE: And reality was as beautiful as those names.

GOLDSCHMIDT: A class from a girls' school. We'd been on an outing to Rome. Or it could have been Naples.

GABRIELE: Let's wake up, Grandfather, in Naples or Rome.

GOLDSCHMIDT: Naples or Rome, that's right. We were in the catacombs and couldn't find the exit.

GABRIELE: *(pensively)* Why do I know this already?

GOLDSCHMIDT: I can tell you.

GABRIELE: Because it's the reality, you mean?

GOLDSCHMIDT: Because of the illustrated paper. One of those old numbers Frau Winter brought us. A report about the catacombs, remember?

GABRIELE: *(almost in tears)* I don't want to remember.

GOLDSCHMIDT: It was about a school outing, a group of girls who lost their way in the passages. Would you prefer that to being here?

GABRIELE: I should prefer it.

GOLDSCHMIDT: Yes, of course you would.

GABRIELE: Recollections of the illustrated paper! Is that all?

GOLDSCHMIDT: No, it isn't. For at the same time we were from Berlin, from this house, this flat.

GABRIELE: *(furious)* Oh, your overflowing imagination! A nice cheerful story you're telling me!

GOLDSCHMIDT: When I was seventeen I saved up my sarcasms.

GABRIELE: What for? I can't make myself more stupid than I am. Can't you understand that I'd like to forget about us, if only for a moment?

GOLDSCHMIDT: I do understand.

GABRIELE: And yet?

GOLDSCHMIDT: Did I say yet?

GABRIELE: You meant it, anyway.

GOLDSCHMIDT: There's no time left for dreams, Gabriele.

GABRIELE: No time left, at seventeen?

GOLDSCHMIDT: That dream of mine seemed like my last. There could be no others after that.

GABRIELE: *(decisively)* Tell it to me.

GOLDSCHMIDT: It's the flavour of the dream. It lies on my tongue like a final word. There's very little to tell.

GABRIELE: Was it in the catacombs, or Berlin?

GOLDSCHMIDT: We'd left Berlin, and were approaching the frontier.

GABRIELE: I don't want to insult your imagination again. It unearths old magazines and settles in dingy flats. And now —

GOLDSCHMIDT: And now — it can think of nothing better than Siegfried Israel Hirschfeld and Edith Sarah Hirschfeld.

GABRIELE: So you dreamed of the Hirschfelds! How could that leave a pleasant taste in your mouth!

GOLDSCHMIDT: We'd reached the frontier.

GABRIELE: We had? Oh dear.

GOLDSCHMIDT: And wrote a postcard to a girl called Gabriele.

GABRIELE: Gabriele Sarah Goldschmidt.

GOLDSCHMIDT: And to her grandfather, saying that all had gone well.

GABRIELE: The postcard the Hirschfelds were going to send us. It should have arrived by now, incidentally. I expect Frau Winter has got it in her handbag.

GOLDSCHMIDT: But then —

GABRIELE: Speak, my ingenious grandparent. Let your ideas come tumbling out, give free play to your gnome-like fancies. Yesterday's war communiqué, perhaps, or Frau Winter's ration card? Why don't you go on?

GOLDSCHMIDT: Then there was something I can't quite recall.

GABRIELE: You cried out in your sleep.

GOLDSCHMIDT: I think they were looking for us in the catacombs.

GABRIELE: Or in Berlin, or at the frontier?

GOLDSCHMIDT: They found us. I don't know whether it was a good thing or a bad thing that they found us.

GABRIELE: But you cried out.

GOLDSCHMIDT: Something bad must have happened at that point.

GABRIELE: Isn't it the worst possible thing anyway, to be found?

GOLDSCHMIDT: What was it? I can't remember. Only the bitter taste has remained.

(A clock strikes far away)

GABRIELE: — five, six.

GOLDSCHMIDT: It's getting dark.

GABRIELE: You say that because it's just struck six. Is there anything else but darkness, ever? Different shades of it, at best. You'd never notice them.

GOLDSCHMIDT: Possibly.

GABRIELE: Nothing provokes you. No feelings, no needs. I'm hungry, for instance.

GOLDSCHMIDT: Frau Winter will soon be back.

GABRIELE: Because it's six o'clock.

GOLDSCHMIDT: It isn't altogether a bad thing that I so rarely feel hungry.

GABRIELE: Grandfather, Robert Israel Goldschmidt!

GOLDSCHMIDT: What?

GABRIELE: I hate you for not being more hungry.

GOLDSCHMIDT: I know you do.

GABRIELE: You don't know anything of the kind. Because it isn't true.

GOLDSCHMIDT: Perhaps it is true at times. I'm often afraid of that: if you lock people up, they get vicious.

GABRIELE: If only I knew that I had the time to get vicious. In that case I'm sure I shouldn't. Well just a little spot or two. Imagine how virtuous we could be, Grandfather, with half a century ahead of us!

GOLDSCHMIDT: Yes, child.

GABRIELE: Now I'm going to black out the window.

GOLDSCHMIDT: That's a good idea.

GABRIELE: It's not a good idea. It's utterly senseless. And I've just noticed that I can no longer do anything without announcing it first. I think if I were to meet myself I'd find myself intolerable.

GOLDSCHMIDT: That would be true of anyone.

GABRIELE: Oh, these words of wisdom! Lessons from the school of life! Take any inane platitude and generalize it, and you're a wiseacre. All's well that ends well. Who said that? Probably someone who was hanging from the gallows.

(Sirens. Air Raid Warning)

GOLDSCHMIDT: The third warning today.

GABRIELE: Three's a lucky number. Don't call any day good before evening. It all fits. Especially for us, when we're asleep in the day-time and awake at night. I'm going to see whether the fire buckets have been filled.

GOLDSCHMIDT: You can rely on Frau Winter.

GABRIELE: And, besides it makes no difference. But I'm going all the same. These little duties give a rhythm to our lives and maintain our sense of order.

GOLDSCHMIDT: Go on, then, and don't chatter so much.

GABRIELE: Am I getting on your nerves at last? Just wait while I quote old Goethe: What makes time fly? Activity! Just about as much imagination as you. He never had an inkling of all the other possible ways of making extravagant hopes: I'll be back in a minute.

(She leaves the room quietly. The door creaks slightly.)

GOLDSCHMIDT: A few minutes' solitude. Could use them to consider whether to put on a tie or not, for example. Does one need a tie when they come to fetch one? Perhaps one does, perhaps it's important. Perhaps everything depends on whether you're wearing one. Or not wearing one. That's something one ought to think about, alone and quickly, for it will be today. Today. Not one of those days between yesterday and tomorrow, but Land's End, the furthest promontory, Finisterre. From below the taste of salt is blown on to your lips, the ultimate taste, you know there is no other.

(GABRIELE returns)

GABRIELE: The water buckets are all right.

GOLDSCHMIDT: And otherwise?

GABRIELE: Most probably the only thing in the world that is all right.

GOLDSCHMIDT: I didn't mean anything so sweeping. Any disturbance in the house?

GABRIELE: Nothing unusual.

(The bell rings)

GABRIELE: Apart from a little visit.

GOLDSCHMIDT: *(whispering)* The hall porter. Or the Air Raid Warden.

GABRIELE: The hall porter. I know his way of ringing the bell. He's wondering where Frau Winter has got to.

GOLDSCHMIDT: Perhaps he wants to tell her that the raid's a heavy one.

GABRIELE: I should have turned on the wireless.

GOLDSCHMIDT: God forbid, Gabriele.

GABRIELE: Oh yes. I know the rules of our game. Keep the stakes low, so that you can't lose much.

GOLDSCHMIDT: Do you hear? He's going down again.

GABRIELE: But every time the bell rings I'm tempted to open the door. Seriously, Grandfather, that's what I want: to see and to be seen. Once and for all.

GOLDSCHMIDT: Do you know what that would mean?

GABRIELE: Careful does it. Look after the pennies — I know. But I have a suspicion that even the pennies are fakes, let alone the pounds.

GOLDSCHMIDT: The world doesn't consist only of counterfeiters.

GABRIELE: Of what else, then?

GOLDSCHMIDT: And you're not serious about all this.

GABRIELE: I'm quite serious about my wishes.

GOLDSCHMIDT: Keep them a little longer, Gabriele.

GABRIELE: Till they've dried up. A collection of dried plants, to be offered up to the Lord with a genuflection. See how virtuous I was, how thrifty!
(Even during these last words a sound of motors. Anti-aircraft fire. Distant bomb explosions.)

GOLDSCHMIDT: High explosive bombs.

GABRIELE: Frau Hirschfeld said she'd go mad if she had to endure another raid in this flat. A kind and tactful way of saying good-bye to us.

GOLDSCHMIDT: I've told you before —

GABRIELE: We can't use the shelter any more than she could.

GOLDSCHMIDT: Frau Hirschfeld's nerves are very bad.

GABRIELE: It doesn't do to have bad nerves when you're trying to cross into Switzerland in the dead of night.

GOLDSCHMIDT: They'll have got over by now.

GABRIELE: And I too have a strong inclination to go mad.

GOLDSCHMIDT: Last night, it was.

GABRIELE: But what about us? I'm seventeen. I haven't lived yet.

GOLDSCHMIDT: To be in Switzerland. At Schaffhausen. Or already in Zürich.

GABRIELE: Didn't you dream they'd been found?

GOLDSCHMIDT: The girls from Viterbo.

GABRIELE: A form outing, wasn't it? Perhaps girls of my own age. In the evening they went out with their arms linked, in twos and threes, through the main street of Viterbo.

35

GOLDSCHMIDT: The previous week there had been a guest tenor at the town theatre.

GABRIELE: *(astonished)* What did you say?

GOLDSCHMIDT: They're talking about him and giggling. It's the evening before their outing to Rome. The square in front of the theatre. A fine evening.

GABRIELE: All your own work, Grandfather?

GOLDSCHMIDT: One lives and learns.

GABRIELE: You astonish me.

(The aeroplanes are now nearer.)

GOLDSCHMIDT: The tenor occurred to me at the same time as my tie.

GABRIELE: *(laughs)*

GOLDSCHMIDT: You know my tie. Blue and red stripes.

GABRIELE: It's quite pretty.

GOLDSCHMIDT: I wish I knew whether I should put it on.

GABRIELE: *(laughing)* Why not?

GOLDSCHMIDT: So you think I should. When I was Pietro Bottari I wore a tie too.

GABRIELE: Did you?

GOLDSCHMIDT: That's hardly encouraging. I wonder what the girls feel like now.

GABRIELE: Very much as I do. Or just a little better. At least there are no bombs over their heads.

GOLDSCHMIDT: Don't listen to them. Think of the catacombs and the girls from Viterbo.

GABRIELE: *(pensively)* I can picture them very clearly. They've all put on their best clothes for the outing. Pink, quite a few of them, some blue, yellow, and one in white. Lovely dresses with collars and belts, and necklaces which no one now can admire.

(The noises of the air raid suddenly cease.)

2

IN THE CATACOMBS

BOTTARI: We must save the candle. Blow it out, Bianca.

BIANCA: Won't it last until they find us?

BOTTARI: Of course it would last, but...

BIANCA: I'll blow it out.

MARIA: They're searching for us already.

LUCIA: Perhaps it will be some time before they find us. What if we miss the last train back?

MARIA: What would our parents say?

LUCIA: That we're coming home tomorrow morning. *(Laughter)* I think it's an interesting experience.

BIANCA: I don't. I'm afraid.

BOTTARI: Afraid? Nonsense.

LUCIA: You see?

BOTTARI: But I should like to know how such a thing could happen. I was the last. Who was the first to come in?

MARIA: Wasn't it you? Lucia?

LUCIA: I was the third or fourth.

BOTTARI: Who was in front of you?

LUCIA: Oh, they kept changing.

BOTTARI: How could we possibly lose sight of the people in front of us, and of the priest? *(Silence)* Who was in front when we noticed it?

LUCIA: I think we had stopped for a moment and we were all together.

BOTTARI: Why had you stopped?

LUCIA: Because all of a sudden we couldn't see anyone ahead of us.

BOTTARI: So none of you was at the front?

BIANCA: It's too late to be sure of it now.

BOTTARI: I see. That means it's my responsibility.

BIANCA: It certainly wasn't your fault, Signor Bottari. You were right at the back.

BOTTARI: Your parents will hardly care whether I was at the front or the back.

LUCIA: I shall tell my parents that it wasn't your fault.

BIANCA: So shall I.

MARIA: All of us shall. You can count on us, Signor Bottari.

BOTTARI: It was my idea to visit the catacombs. They will hold that against me.

ANTONIA: Why bother to talk about it? What's happened anyway? We've lost our way, and shall get home a few hours late. That's all.

LENA: Antonia's right.

MARIA: What's the time?

BOTTARI: A quarter to seven.

MARIA: In that case they must find us soon. The last train leaves at eight.

LENA: Quiet! I think I heard someone call.

37

Silence

The words that follow are spoken very softly

LUCIA: Antonia!

ANTONIA: Is it you, Lucia?

LUCIA: I want to tell you something.

ANTONIA: What is it?

LUCIA: It was me.

ANTONIA: What was?

LUCIA: I was at the front. I turned into another passage on purpose; no one noticed it. Do you think that was bad?

ANTONIA: No. But why did you turn off?

LUCIA: I don't know. I was bored. I'm bored by everything, the whole of life. Can you understand that?

ANTONIA: Yes, I can.

LUCIA: But now I'm afraid.

ANTONIA: Nonsense.

LUCIA: What if they never find us?

ANTONIA: Of course they'll find us.

(The following aloud)

BOTTARI: Who's that whispering all the time? Can't you keep quiet?

LENA: What's the time now, Signor Bottari?

BOTTARI: *(after hesitating briefly)* Wasn't it a quarter to seven when you last asked me?

LENA: Has your watch stopped?

BOTTARI: Does anyone here know the time?

Silence.

LENA: No, I don't think anyone does.

BIANCA: Perhaps it was later even when we last asked you.

MARIA: In that case we shan't catch our train.

BOTTARI: We shall spend the night in the waiting room. I can think of worse things.

LUCIA: Do you think that perhaps we should move on?

ANTONIA: Leave that to Signor Bottari.

MARIA: *(suddenly bursts into tears)*

BOTTARI: *(irritated)* What's the matter? What are you crying for?

BIANCA: What's wrong with you? Maria?

LENA: *(tittering)* She's hungry.

MARIA: I'm not hungry.

BOTTARI: What is it, then?

MARIA: What if they never find us?

BOTTARI: Don't talk such rubbish.

ANTONIA: Let's finish the chocolate. And then we'll lie down and sleep.

BIANCA: I can't lie down in this filth. I'm wearing a white frock.

LENA: Well, stand, then. We shall all get dirty down here.

BIANCA: I'm not going to spoil my frock. I got it specially for the outing. Who would think of lying down here. It's damp and cold, and there's a draft. Aren't the walls dripping?

BOTTARI: That's your imagination.

LUCIA: Why don't we sing.

LENA: So that we won't be able to hear anything?

LUCIA: So that you won't get depressed.

BOTTARI: No one here is depressed. We're all quite cheerful, aren't we.

ANTONIA: *(when no one has replied)* Of course we are.

BOTTARI: After all, it's an adventure. And you girls are usually keen enough on adventures! Just think what stories you'll be able to tell at home, to your parents and brothers and sisters. All at once you've become the most interesting girls in Viterbo. Isn't that worth while? Your names will be in the papers.

MARIA: So it's as bad as that.

BOTTARI: Adventures are often uncomfortable.

LENA: *(to herself)* I know of some that are very comfortable.
(One of them titters)

BOTTARI: What are you laughing about?

BIANCA: Lena says she knows of some adventures that are very comfortable.

LENA: *(quickly)* In any case this is not one of them. It's pretty hard where I'm sitting.

LUCIA: Now my parents have just come to the station to meet me.

MARIA: And mine too.

LUCIA: And then they'll think that we're coming on the last train.

ANTONIA: The last train arrives at Viterbo just before midnight. All our parents will be at the station.

LUCIA: They don't yet know that we shan't be on the last one either.

BOTTARI: Be quiet now.

LUCIA: Why did I ever begin it?

BOTTARI: I'm going to shout. That at least can do no harm. *(He calls out)* Halloh! — Halloh! — Halloh! — *(His calls fade out)*
Pause

3

ALL CLEAR SIGNAL

GABRIELE: *(locking the door)* That's that.

GOLDSCHMIDT: All clear?

GABRIELE: All things have an end, except —

GOLDSCHMIDT: That's enough!

GABRIELE: Or would you rather I said: 'What is not yet, can still be'?

GOLDSCHMIDT: I had a terrible hope, Gabriele.

GABRIELE: You're going one better than me, then.

GOLDSCHMIDT: That I shall be spared the worry of thinking about my tie.

GABRIELE: I don't understand that joke.

GOLDSCHMIDT: And it's a bad one too.

GABRIELE: That's the reason.

GOLDSCHMIDT: The reason is the bad taste that won't leave my mouth.

GABRIELE: Your dreams are due to hunger. What's become of Frau Winter?

GOLDSCHMIDT: Held up by the raid.

GABRIELE: She could have been here before the raid. What else are clocks for, clocks that strike six? Not a crumb of bread in the bin. I suspect her of dawdling on purpose.

GOLDSCHMIDT: There's nothing she doesn't do for us.

GABRIELE: Up to now we've paid for it.

GOLDSCHMIDT: Paid for it? What, for the danger she's incurred? How much do you reckon that is worth?

GABRIELE: And in saying that, one ought to roll one's eyes and fall on one's knees. Oh, I hate them for it, and not only Frau Winter.

GOLDSCHMIDT: No, your grandfather too.

GABRIELE: Everyone.

GOLDSCHMIDT: That's always been the easiest way.

GABRIELE: And myself most of all.

GOLDSCHMIDT: How pathetic — just as if you were no older than — than you are.

GABRIELE: *(amused)* And my stupidities?

GOLDSCHMIDT: Just as though you were still learning to talk.

GABRIELE: And yet I feel as if I were seventy! No, a hundred and seventy! Oh, Grandfather, dear old Grandfather, you're quite right.

GOLDSCHMIDT: What about?

GABRIELE: We're almost the same age. Those fifty years make no difference, since every day spent in this place is like a year.

GOLDSCHMIDT: More than that.

GABRIELE: And the time before, when they beat Father to death and took away Mother? Aunt Esther counts too, and the unknown young man in the flat next to ours who cried out for help. It adds up to several centuries. Look at me clearly: I'm a shrivelled, ancient crone.

GOLDSCHMIDT: But you still have your wishes?

GABRIELE: Transformed into a seventeen-year-old girl, if you like. But what do my wishes amount to? They're all so vague.

GOLDSCHMIDT: To walk in a park at night, perhaps?

GABRIELE: *(serious)* And someone beside me who loves me. No one loves me.

GOLDSCHMIDT: You exaggerate.

GABRIELE: Am I plain?

GOLDSCHMIDT: No.

GABRIELE: But not particularly pretty. A pity! I'd rather be a celebrated beauty. At the opera people turn their glasses toward my box. People stare at me in the street: the Goldschmidt girl.

GOLDSCHMIDT: Gabriele Sarah.

GABRIELE: Wouldn't you think the name attractive enough? Beauty would change everything. It would have a completely new ring: Goldschmidt. And besides —

GOLDSCHMIDT: Quiet!

GABRIELE: Footsteps on the stairs?

GOLDSCHMIDT: *(whispering)* It could be Frau Winter. *(They listen. The door to the flat is opened. Footsteps in the corridor.)*

GABRIELE: Perhaps she's got some fish. Some cod would cheer me up. *(The footsteps halt in front of the door to their room. The door handle is slowly pressed down, the door opens.)*

FRAU WINTER: Ah — you're there.

GOLDSCHMIDT: *(laughing)* That sounds as though you're surprised.

FRAU WINTER: Oh, no, I just said it without thinking. One talks such a lot of nonsense.

GABRIELE: We should be glad to be somewhere else.

GOLDSCHMIDT: Please don't misunderstand Gabriele.

GABRIELE: I didn't mean it that way, we're most grateful to you, and so on.

41

FRAU WINTER: *(affably)* In short, nothing unusual has happened.

GABRIELE: Three raids, two rings on the bell. We understand one another.

GOLDSCHMIDT: And what about you, Frau Winter?

FRAU WINTER: About me?

GOLDSCHMIDT: Something unusual?

FRAU WINTER: No.

GOLDSCHMIDT: You look strained.

GABRIELE: I expect we do, too. There's just been a raid, after all.

FRAU WINTER: Mainly around Lichterfelde, the South End.

GABRIELE: That's a long way off.

GOLDSCHMIDT: Near enough for many.

GABRIELE: A pronouncement that should reduce us to solemn silence. Cheer up, Grandfather, it'll be our turn soon.

FRAU WINTER: I'll go and get the supper.

GABRIELE: While I look for suitable proverbs.

GOLDSCHMIDT: It would be better to help Frau Winter.

GABRIELE: You know she doesn't want me to. It's too close to the passage door.

FRAU WINTER: There's cod for supper.

GABRIELE: Well, what do you say to that, Grandfather. My premonitions are better than yours.

GOLDSCHMIDT: More tasty, anyhow.

FRAU WINTER: *(as she leaves the room)* Here you are! The card from the Hirschfelds.

GABRIELE: Give it to me, Grandfather.

GOLDSCHMIDT: *(reading)* 'Holiday greeting from Richard and Clara. We are well.'

GABRIELE: *(laughs)* Richard and Clara.

GOLDSCHMIDT: The pre-arranged words.

GABRIELE: And a lovely little view into the bargain. Something we didn't pre-arrange. It never rains but it pours.

GOLDSCHMIDT: Let me see it.

GABRIELE: 'Singen, with a view of the Hohentwiel peak.'

GOLDSCHMIDT: So they've got as far as Singen.

GABRIELE: Have you ever heard of Singen? A very unlikely name. And Hohentwiel, with a t and a w. There's no such place.

GOLDSCHMIDT: They must have crossed the border by now.

GABRIELE: If only we could find out! You know, Grandfather, I've been thinking all day that the arrival of the postcard will be an omen. A sign that we shall come through.

GOLDSCHMIDT: Yes.

GABRIELE: Or don't you think so, Grandfather?

GOLDSCHMIDT: Why wasn't Frau Winter pleased about the card?

GABRIELE: Wasn't she pleased?

GOLDSCHMIDT: My impression was that she wasn't pleased. She gave it to us last of all. And without any further comment.

GABRIELE: I expect that she wishes that we were in Switzerland too.

GOLDSCHMIDT: I'm sure she does, the kind soul.

GABRIELE: Or in Jericho, for that matter. I don't blame the kind soul.

GOLDSCHMIDT: Are you starting again, Gabriele?

GABRIELE: And does it matter in the least whether Frau Winter is pleased? We are pleased. All is well. The girls from Viterbo will be found.

GOLDSCHMIDT: They were not found.

GABRIELE: Oh?

GOLDSCHMIDT: They never returned to the light of day.

GABRIELE: *(after hesitating briefly)* I don't believe that anyone can get lost in the catacombs. A fiction fit only for the readers of illustrated magazines. No. Grandfather, it all ends as happily as our story is turning out.

GOLDSCHMIDT: Our story?

GABRIELE: A red-letter day of the first order.

GOLDSCHMIDT: Because of the cod, above all.

GABRIELE: Don't be sarcastic.

GOLDSCHMIDT: And then the postcard about which Frau Winter is not pleased.

GABRIELE: As I said, I am pleased. And I had the feeling that I could save the girls from Viterbo. Today I have the power and the right.

GOLDSCHMIDT: Use it, then Gabriele. So they're being searched for?

GABRIELE: They are.

GOLDSCHMIDT: One of the monks —

GABRIELE: No, it should be better than that.

GOLDSCHMIDT: In what way?

GABRIELE: To put it precisely, it should make you cry.

GOLDSCHMIDT: *(laughing)* No monks, then, no fire engines, no police?

GABRIELE: No, no kind of professional rescue party.

GOLDSCHMIDT: Love, I suppose?

GABRIELE: That's it.

GOLDSCHMIDT: Love will find them, then.

GABRIELE: That's what I'm saying.

GOLDSCHMIDT: Even if no one finds them.

GABRIELE: What do you mean?

GOLDSCHMIDT: Love has no ropes and no lamps and can pull no one out of the maze. It is powerless.

GABRIELE: That isn't true. I am making it powerful.

GOLDSCHMIDT: Make it lucky.

GABRIELE: Luck is no accident, I've learnt. Listen!

4

IN THE CATACOMBS

LUCIA: Are you asleep, Antonia?

ANTONIA: Aren't you either, Lucia?

LUCIA: I've got so much to think about. What are you thinking?

ANTONIA: I don't know. I don't know what to do with so much time. It frightens me.

LUCIA: It's my thoughts that frighten me.

ANTONIA: I don't even know whether I have any thoughts.

LUCIA: For instance I'm thinking — Are you thinking of your father, Antonia?

ANTONIA: I'm thinking of my father.

LUCIA: And of your mother too?

ANTONIA: My mother too.

LUCIA: And of your sisters?

ANTONIA: I'm thinking of my sisters too.

LUCIA: And who else?

ANTONIA: Who else? *(After a while, calmly)* Of Pietro Bottari, our teacher.

LUCIA: Oh!

ANTONIA: Are you satisfied?

LUCIA: And Bottari? Does he know?

ANTONIA: How could he? I've only known it myself since you asked me?

LUCIA: Are you joking, Antonia?

ANTONIA: Think what you like.

LUCIA: I'd like to be friends with you, Antonia.

44

ANTONIA: Is there still time for that?

LUCIA: I'd like to be able to talk to you, to tell you everything.

ANTONIA: Well, tell me, then.

LUCIA: If you think of one person more than anyone else —

ANTONIA: Well?

LUCIA: Does that mean you love him?

ANTONIA: How should I know? You'd have to ask Margarita. She knows all the boys in Viterbo.

LUCIA: That's just why I expect she doesn't know.

ANTONIA: And you think that we two know better?

LUCIA: Don't be flippant. Just tell me: does that mean you love him?

ANTONIA: One might suppose so.

LUCIA: *(triumphant)* In that case I love Emilio Fostino.

ANTONIA: Oh, yes?

LUCIA: You don't seem to be impressed.

ANTONIA: I don't know him.

LUCIA: He's seventeen, apprentice in a joinery, a few houses away from ours. And we're almost strangers.

ANTONIA: There's nothing wrong with his age.

LUCIA: One day, just in front of our house, a chest of drawers fell off his cart. I couldn't help laughing.

ANTONIA: And he was enchanted?

LUCIA: He was furious. It worries me now.

ANTONIA: Yes, I've heard of fury and of laughter. And who could prove that it might not begin with the upsetting of a chest of drawers?

LUCIA: Do you think so, Antonia?

ANTONIA: *(sighs)*

LUCIA: Or aren't you listening?

ANTONIA: *(distressed)* Oh yes, I'm listening.

LUCIA: What are you thinking?

ANTONIA: I'm not thinking. I'd like to know what Bottari is thinking.

LUCIA: He's asleep.

ANTONIA: Are you so sure?

NO SCENE

BOTTARI: A game of billiards with the Lord Mayor, on a weekday, five in the afternoon. One agrees to meet, one belongs. It is the hour when Angelica visits Signor Giraldi. One knows and doesn't know, according to one's convenience. Outside, in the dusty sunshine, the

45

headmaster is passing by. He waves through the window, and will be with us in a moment. Mario, an espresso, please.

The weather? Your wife? The half-light in the billiard room is like the town's respect. 45 years old, a schoolteacher, married, without children. Done nothing to cause a stir, either in Heaven or on earth. The balls collide, not many voices, the sounds of darkness. I've always lived in caves. My partner chalks his cue and hopes he will make a break. The figures add up on the board, the final result is fixed. Have attained what there was to be attained, a place in the dark. In billiard rooms, holes and corners, catacombs — hail to you, my caves, my ultimate home! I have come to you. The deceptions vanish, chair, match, and clock; there is no gap where they were, darkness easily fills their place. My knees slightly drawn up, my head leaning against the stone, a posture for going to sleep, a middling idyll, just uncomfortable enough to permit some satisfaction.

The red and white balls, the patterns they trace on the glaring green. Whom is the Lord Mayor playing today? Mario, the bill, please. It is the moment when Angelica slips into her shoes again. The exercise books have been corrected, the coffee has been drunk, not a single head appears in the lamplight. The moment, missed until now, to die inconspicuously, uncommunicatively above all. Never felt any need to be conspicuous, and now there is the breathing around me, fifteen-fold. A rustling, a sighing, starched petticoats or sleep. Have attained what there is to be attained: a place in guilt. Fifteen-fold guilt, no part of it vanishes, not an empty space for darkness to fill.

Chosen, a billiards champion, with those distinctions which are permitted. Why? I could owe them the price of my coffee, and yet remain respected as before. Lived as it was most convenient to live, but who doesn't? Committed the sins of indifference and of melancholy, who knows them? Angelica perhaps, I make an exception of her. She knows that everyone else has advantages which I lack. Especially Giraldi, I suppose, my colleague, Giraldi. He will organize a rescue party for us, he's splendid at organizing, the fool, and he will succeed too in not finding us. The waiter opens the door. A draught of fresh air, thy breath, O Lord, that blows me away; I can feel it clearly. Good evening, Signor Bottari. I have been noticed — that in itself is the verdict. I understand it, I

46

am in agreement, I accept. But only for myself, not for those who are with me.

Put the chairs on the tables, put out the light, — Oh, it isn't quite as simple as that, Lord Mayor. Or what is your opinion?

IN THE CATACOMBS

LUCIA: Come closer, Antonia.

ANTONIA: Bottari is talking in his sleep.

LUCIA: Put your arm around me.

ANTONIA: That better?

LUCIA: Yes, I'm less afraid now. Do you remember what the priest said: dust?

ANTONIA: I remember.

LUCIA: And the remains of bones, mixed up together.

ANTONIA: What else could he say?

LUCIA: It doesn't upset you?

ANTONIA: It was a conducted tour, not a prophecy.

LUCIA: Or both? Mixed up — like the dust with the bones. Oh I'd rather have grass, Antonia.

ANTONIA: Grass? Green fields? I can do without them. This dust is the very thing for me.

LUCIA: For you. How lucky you are!

ANTONIA: Luckier than you?

LUCIA: Only a few steps away from him.

ANTONIA: Further than Viterbo. Distances alter, don't you find? Your Emilio, for instance —

LUCIA: Yes?

ANTONIA: Is only incidentally far away — more easily reached, really, and closer to happiness —

LUCIA: Than Bottari?

ANTONIA: *(pensively)* It's a kind of physics with quite different laws.

LUCIA: Catacomb physics.

ANTONIA: *(without paying attention to her)* Some sections are missing entirely. No Heat, no Optics, what a thought! But Magnetism, oh yes, and the Theory of Melancholy —

LUCIA: I could contribute a formula to that myself! The suppressed sigh or the expression 'When I'm back in Viterbo.'

ANTONIA: Not an easy one to substitute in this equation. And what sign would it have? plus or minus?

47

LUCIA: *(suddenly)* Antonia, I'm going to communicate with Emilio.

ANTONIA: Yes, of course, Lucia. And there's a letter-box up by the entrance.

LUCIA: What would that be doing in our science? Didn't you say, different laws? Emilio! Supposing I were to think about him now with all my strength?

ANTONIA: Oh dear, what have I started?

LUCIA: Couldn't he sense it?

ANTONIA: Of course. You'll show him the way.

LUCIA: And why not?

ANTONIA: Three left, three right. All you need is a crochet pattern.

LUCIA: All the way to us. It would be an experiment, applied physics.

ANTONIA: Try it.

LUCIA: From him to me and from me to him thoughts travel like waves of sound.

ANTONIA: You're making me laugh, Lucia.

LUCIA: As long as he can hear them he's on his way to us.

ANTONIA: I hope he knows it too. He's only a beginner, remember.

LUCIA: It only takes a matter of minutes to learn this science.

ANTONIA: How I wish you were right. Then think of Emilio. *(Sighing)* Meanwhile I shall think of Bottari.

LUCIA: A lot of nonsense. I know it is.

ANTONIA: Sense or nonsense, it's all much the same in our position. Altogether there's something comic about it.

LUCIA: I can't see that.

ANTONIA: No one outside would see it either, I imagine. But why shouldn't we? My dear Lucia, you've no idea how silly I think myself. My crush on Bottari! That is, if Bottari isn't a name I've substituted for another.

LUCIA: For another?

ANTONIA: Does that make you curious? And I don't even know whether there is any other. But there is a Signora Bottari.

LUCIA: They say that Signora Bottari —

ANTONIA: There's no end to what people will say.

A ROOM IN BOTTARI'S HOUSE

ANGELICA: Are we doing all we can?

GIRALDI: You saw for yourself when we were in Rome. The fire brigade, police, pioneers, search parties. All organized as efficiently as could be.

ANGELICA: I mean us. Are *we* doing all we can?

GIRALDI: What can we do, Angelica? In such cases it's not individuals, it's the public services that have to be mobilized. And that's the State's responsibility towards its citizens.

ANGELICA: I'm still speaking about us.

GIRALDI: We must be patient, Angelica.

ANGELICA: In other words —

GIRALDI: It's now five days since it happened. Let's face the facts. The most modern appliances have been used, and several hundred men. You saw them yourself, the serious faces under their helmets and caps, their determination, their devotion to duty; they know what's at stake. Didn't you feel that one could completely rely on them?

ANGELICA: Yes, and if you count in the sun on their helmets, it's bound to be a success. All the movement orders, the disposition of commandos and patrols, one can rely on those. But on us, Lorenzo?

GIRALDI: Let me finish. Even this great effort has been unsuccessful till now. The catacombs are very intricate, no one knows the full extent of all the passages and besides — they have no provisions.

ANGELICA: Are those prospects meant to console me?

GIRALDI: Of course not. I'm only saying that we ourselves could do much less, or nothing at all. Even in Rome. You go there —

ANGELICA: And pretend you're doing something.

GIRALDI: There's nothing to be done but wait.

ANGELICA: For what?

GIRALDI: For what?

ANGELICA: Face facts, that's what you said. Well, what are the facts? Is the sun still flashing on those helmets? What thoughts do all those watching faces now express?

GIRALDI: You mean our relationship?

ANGELICA: Which is beginning to be the main topic at Viterbo. Giraldi and Signora Bottari, Signora Bottari and Giraldi — only that, and endlessly.

GIRALDI: Well it's a topic that makes me happy.

ANGELICA: Facts, please, the facts as they are, without adornment. All the colours have faded.

GIRALDI: So soon?

ANGELICA: You have the opportunity to visit me undisturbed. A happy chance that was not to be foreseen. My husband — shall we say, gone away for an indefinite period. Perhaps for ever. Lorenzo, what more could we ask for?

GIRALDI: *(uncertain)* Well?

ANGELICA: *(hoarsely)* But it's this voice I always hear, saying: a few more days, a few more days, then you'll have some peace, then you'll be free: inside, you understand, where there won't be any more faces and no sun on helmets. Tell me what you're waiting for, Lorenzo.

GIRALDI: You.

ANGELICA: That's reasonable, isn't it? A plain fact. As simple as that. A twist of fate — *(more softly)* something ordained by God.

GIRALDI: We do not know His thoughts. But in so far as we do know them —

ANGELICA: They're comforting.

GIRALDI: Oh let's stop being metaphysical.

ANGELICA: And do what?

GIRALDI: Forget, live for each other.

ANGELICA: Is that all?

GIRALDI: Try to get over it.

ANGELICA: That's right. But where?

GIRALDI: Here, and nowhere else. Use all this precious time for our love. Without distractions. Hair, eyebrows, skin, kisses — cataclysms enough!

ANGELICA: Enough, Lorenzo.

GIRALDI: What do you mean?

ANGELICA: Leave me now.

GIRALDI: I don't understand you.

ANGELICA: I want to be left alone.

GIRALDI: Are you reproaching me?

ANGELICA: Myself. I should have stayed in Rome, that was the least I could do. I left my anxiety to the fire brigade, and to the police. My tears were crocodile tears. Waiting there, before the catacombs, was tedious. Oh, I'm properly on my own trail now, I assure you, and it leads straight through a thicket to a hidden swamp — a few bubbles of marsh gas still rising, that's all that's left of me.

GIRALDI: Angelica you're hurting me.

ANGELICA: Hurting you? Is that all?

(A ring on the bell)

GIRALDI: A moment longer!

ANGELICA: No, not a moment longer!

(She leaves the room, through the passage, and opens the door.)

EMILIO: May I have a word with you, Signora?

ANGELICA: Have you any news?

EMILIO: No, not news exactly.

ANGELICA: Then what do you want? Who are you?

EMILIO: My name is Emilio Fostini, and I work in Ruggiero's joinery.

ANGELICA: I can't say that I know the name.

EMILIO: And it has nothing to do with what I came to see you about.

ANGELICA: Well?

EMILIO: But I thought that if Signora Bottari comes to the door I shall simply say it, and she'll understand.

ANGELICA: Well? What is it?

EMILIO: A thousand lire. *(After a pause)* I wanted to ask you to lend me a thousand lire, so that I can go to Rome.

ANGELICA: Is there a member of your family among them?

EMILIO: Oh no. It's just that I've met one of the girls, casually. Forgive me, now that it comes to the point, it does seem rather ridiculous, to me, too.

ANGELICA: You mean now that I've opened the door and you've seen me?

EMILIO: No, no, I didn't mean that.

ANGELICA: Wait — wait a minute.

EMILIO: *(calling after her)* You see, it might just have worked — you looked at me in such a way — you'll get it all back, Signora, as sure as —

ANGELICA: *(coming back)* I'll go with you.

EMILIO: *(happy)* As sure as we are to find them.

(The door slams. In the open air.)

EMILIO: When I woke up last night, I knew it — only since last night — I suddenly knew it, I sat up in bed and there it was! *(Breathlessly and as though fading into the distance)* And I thought, too, you can't leave everything to the fire brigade and the police.

IN THE CATACOMBS

LENA: How long? What do you think?

BIANCA: Five days.

MARIA: Six.

LUCIA: Or four.

BOTTARI: When day and night are the same it's easy to make a mistake.

51

LENA: And not only then. *(More softly)* Teachers especially.

BOTTARI: One loses one's sense of time. I don't think it's more than three days at the most.

MARIA: If it's easy to make a mistake, it could be eight days too.

LENA: If only we had some light.

ANTONIA: We still shouldn't know how long.

LENA: We could play cards.

ANTONIA: If we had any!

LUCIA: If, and that's an end of it. Who can still think of something without an if?

LENA: How long does it take to die of starvation? Without any if.

BIANCA: The world record is 45 days.

MARIA: In that case we've got plenty of time.

BOTTARI: Don't talk such wicked nonsense!

LENA: I'm afraid I can think of nothing else any more. Red tomatoes, spaghetti and parmesan. Usually I can't stand parmesan.

BIANCA: Maize biscuits and coffee.

ANTONIA: It makes no difference how long we've been here; we shall be rescued. And every day brings it nearer.

MARIA: I can no longer believe that.

LUCIA: Who said that?

MARIA: I, Maria. And I shall say it again: I no longer believe it.

OTHERS: I don't believe it either.

ANTONIA: But I believe it.

LUCIA: So do I.

LENA: Only two?

LUCIA: Why don't you speak, Signor Bottari?

BOTTARI: Because I have to listen, and because it's so hard with all your chatter.

ANTONIA: What are you listening for?

LENA: You're always hearing something, Signor Bottari.

BIANCA: Signor Bottari has already said, when day and night are the same it's easy to make a mistake.

(They titter.)

BOTTARI: Quiet!

(Silence.)

BOTTARI: I thought I heard my wife calling me.

LENA: *(laughs)*

ANTONIA: What are you laughing for, Lena? Goose!

52

LENA: Goose yourself, you stuck-up thing!

LUCIA: I thought I heard Emilio call.

BIANCA: Who's Emilio?

MARIA: Emilio!

(Laughter.)

LENA: There's no accounting for tastes.

MARIA: *(sarcastically)* Let's all listen! Perhaps in that case we shall all —

BOTTARI: Quiet!

(Voices are heard calling very far away.)

BOTTARI: Can't you hear it?

LENA: No. I can't hear a thing, much as I should like to.

BIANCA: Not a thing.

LUCIA: But I hear it.

(Commotion.)

BOTTARI: *(calls out)* Anybody there? *(More loudly)* Hullo, is anybody there?

ANGELICA: *(far away)* We're coming.

EMILIO: *(somewhat nearer)* We're coming, Signor Bottari!

GIRLS: *(set up a confused shrieking)*

LUCIA: Emilio!

BIANCA: Who's Emilio?

LENA: I hope they've brought us some food.

MARIA: The monks, you mean?

(Laughter)

LENA: They've found us.

ANTONIA: They've found us.

EMILIO: *(even nearer)* We're coming — we're coming —

(Silence)

5

GOLDSCHMIDT: Saved.

GABRIELE: Yes.

GOLDSCHMIDT: That's nice to hear.

GABRIELE: How do you mean, Grandfather?

GOLDSCHMIDT: And saved by whom?

GABRIELE: Wasn't it quite simple?

GOLDSCHMIDT: By Emilio, Emilio Fostini.

GABRIELE: *(shyly)* That's what I called him.

GOLDSCHMIDT: And all very nicely invented. The name, and he's a joiner's apprentice, the chest of drawers that falls off the cart, the thousand lire —

GABRIELE: Well? What are you driving at? Saved by whom, you asked?

GOLDSCHMIDT: Not by Emilio, Gabriele. By you.

GABRIELE: *(unsure)* Because I invented the story.

GOLDSCHMIDT: That's it, invented. And well, too. So that you hardly notice the trick. One, two, three, and the rabbit jumps out of the hat. Three, two, one, and it's vanished down your sleeve. Or the neck of your frock.

GABRIELE: A rabbit? That would be something, too. But in my case there was no rabbit.

GOLDSCHMIDT: A conjuring trick. But do conjurors tell stories? You made it easy for yourself.

GABRIELE: It was very hard.

GOLDSCHMIDT: True enough, and that's why it was easy. No, this way it's false, the story.

GABRIELE: I shall leave it as it is.

GOLDSCHMIDT: I've got the feeling that you'll have to tell it again.

GABRIELE: Have to? Who can compel me?

(*Enter* FRAU WINTER)

FRAU WINTER: There, then, food's ready.

(The table is laid.)

GABRIELE: Fish!

FRAU WINTER: With potatoes and parsley sauce.

GOLDSCHMIDT: A special day.

FRAU WINTER: *(with meaning)* Better not a special day.

GOLDSCHMIDT: I only meant the cod.

FRAU WINTER: Even if you only meant the cod —

GABRIELE: This time it was you, Grandfather.

GOLDSCHMIDT: I confess and repent.

GABRIELE: And now a bad joke into the bargain. This isn't one of your good days, Grandfather.

FRAU WINTER: At it again! Today of all days.

GABRIELE: This time it was me. That brings our score back to even, back to normal. A day like all the rest. Let's eat.

FRAU WINTER: If only I were hungry.

GOLDSCHMIDT: Um? You too?

GABRIELE: Don't worry. *I'm* ravenous.

(They eat.)

GABRIELE: What was it like in the office today?

GOLDSCHMIDT: Let Frau Winter eat.

FRAU WINTER: Two hours' shorthand. Seventeen letters. Nothing unusual.

GABRIELE: Your table is by the window, and sometimes you look out, don't you, Frau Winter?

FRAU WINTER: Sometimes I do, absentmindedly. Brown uniforms, grey uniforms, slate-blue ones, black ones — it isn't worth it.

GOLDSCHMIDT: Cars, mackintoshes — no, windows really aren't worth while. There are countries where there's a tax on them. Quite right too. Congratulations, incidentally: the parsley sauce. An inexhaustible topic.

FRAU WINTER: Thank you. A recipe of my mother's.

GABRIELE: One ought to write it down, for later. I'm afraid I shall never learn to cook.

FRAU WINTER: *(hurriedly)* And it isn't important either. There are restaurants, cooks, and tins.

GABRIELE: Frau Winter, are there trees in your street?

FRAU WINTER: Yes, plane trees, I think.

GABRIELE: And it's autumn now, isn't it?

GOLDSCHMIDT: The 5th or 6th of October. Silly questions, Gabriele.

FRAU WINTER: The seventh.

GABRIELE: Autumn.

GOLDSCHMIDT: I think we've got that clear.

GABRIELE: And the effect of autumn on plane-trees?

GOLDSCHMIDT: Is yellow leaves. But in your mind, Gabriele? Anyone would think —

FRAU WINTER: Yes, the leaves are yellow now. That's the prettiest thing about the street.

GABRIELE: Really? You say they're yellow now?

FRAU WINTER: I assure you —

GABRIELE: You're giving me courage.

GOLDSCHMIDT: What are you playing at, Gabriele?

GABRIELE: The leaves yellow, and what then?

FRAU WINTER: They fall off, of course.

GABRIELE: They do fall off?

FRAU WINTER: Not yet. Or only one at a time. But soon they'll all be falling.

GABRIELE: You're not saying that just to comfort me?

FRAU WINTER: I can't see anything comforting about it.

GABRIELE: It's certain, then, that the leaves turn yellow and fall? It comes about that way, it happens every year?

GOLDSCHMIDT: One can safely affirm it.

GABRIELE: Thank God!

FRAU WINTER: Did you doubt it?

GABRIELE: I was no longer quite sure whether it really is so, or whether I merely imagined it. There are many things I'm no longer sure about, but I'm afraid to ask. Bombs and prisons, those really exist. But trees? Or an animal called a mole, that lives under the earth and is nearly blind? Or a country called Switzerland? It could well be that they're mere fantasies.

(FRAU WINTER *puts down her fork on the plate.*)

GABRIELE: What's wrong with you, Frau Winter?

FRAU WINTER: I've had enough to eat.

GABRIELE: Nobody here finishes a meal. I've had more than anyone.

FRAU WINTER: Moles do exist, by the way, and so does Switzerland.

GABRIELE: Tell me something else.

FRAU WINTER: Nothing of it is good.

GABRIELE: Don't worry, I've learnt that.

FRAU WINTER: Suddenly there was the alarm. I was on my way home and went into the shelter near the zoo. It was dark. No, really there's nothing to tell you.

GABRIELE: There's the postcard, Frau Winter. Singen, with a view of Hohentwiel.

FRAU WINTER: I saw it.

GABRIELE: We're glad that the Hirschfelds have got away.

FRAU WINTER: Have you finished, Gabriele?

GABRIELE: Yes. And have you, Frau Winter?

FRAU WINTER: Then I'll clear the table.

GABRIELE: Aren't you glad?

FRAU WINTER: Glad?

GABRIELE: Yes.

FRAU WINTER: I'm not glad.

(Silence.)

I talked to someone who saw the Hirschfelds.

GABRIELE: At Singen?

FRAU WINTER: In Berlin.

GABRIELE: Berlin?

FRAU WINTER: The Gestapo prison at Moabit.

GABRIELE: And the postcard?

GOLDSCHMIDT: Is meaningless? They didn't get away?
   (Silence.)

FRAU WINTER: Quiet!

GABRIELE: Footsteps, nothing out of the ordinary. They're passing by.

FRAU WINTER: *(sighs)*

GOLDSCHMIDT: I dreamed last night that I was trying to cross the frontier.

GABRIELE: You were the teacher with those girls from Viterbo. They were found.

GOLDSCHMIDT: We were found, and I cried out in my sleep. Although we were found or because we were found? Gabriele —

GABRIELE: What?

GOLDSCHMIDT: I know it now.

GABRIELE: What do you know?

GOLDSCHMIDT: They asked us where we'd been. I gave them our address.

GABRIELE: Our address?

GOLDSCHMIDT: Without thinking. But then I realized, and I cried out with anguish at the thought that I'd given it away.

GABRIELE: Our address.

FRAU WINTER: That's what I've been thinking about the whole day.

GABRIELE: Now it's you, Frau Winter! A special day indeed: dreams, cod, a postcard from Singen, and our address. What else could there be?

GOLDSCHMIDT: Perhaps it was a mistake, and it wasn't the Hirschfelds.

FRAU WINTER: Perhaps.

GOLDSCHMIDT: And perhaps they won't be asked for our address.

FRAU WINTER: Yes, that could be.

GOLDSCHMIDT: And if they are asked, perhaps they'll give a different address.

FRAU WINTER: Yes.

GABRIELE: So many perhapses, so many possibilities. *(After a pause)* And you don't believe in any of them.

GOLDSCHMIDT: We must leave this house.

FRAU WINTER: Where for?

GABRIELE: Live in the open air. In the forests, for all I care.

FRAU WINTER: Where are your forests?

GOLDSCHMIDT: No passports, and no money to buy false ones.

FRAU WINTER: What do passports amount to, anyway? You've seen how much good they are.

GABRIELE: You've been thinking all day long, Frau Winter, the whole of this special day.

FRAU WINTER: A new hiding place for a few days. Till the danger's past.

GOLDSCHMIDT: Leave here without being seen?

FRAU WINTER: It's more dangerous to stay. For me too, I think.

GABRIELE: Good-bye cod, food without coupons and illustrated weeklies.

GOLDSCHMIDT: You're insufferable, Gabriele.

GABRIELE: Lazy above all, my dear Grandfather, grown lazy here. Frau Winter has spoilt us.

FRAU WINTER: And I don't suppose it will be comfortable exactly.

GABRIELE: You see!

GOLDSCHMIDT: But where else could we hide? We don't know of anyone.

FRAU WINTER: Nor do I know of anyone yet.

GABRIELE: Frau Winter said yet. I always thought she was an archangel.

FRAU WINTER: *(somewhat absent-minded)* With me it's only a question of sleep, of sound sleep for the rest of my life. And I don't know whether I shall have any success. At eight o'clock — what's the time?

GOLDSCHMIDT: Half past seven.

FRAU WINTER: I'm going now. At eight Frau Kallmorgen will be home.

GABRIELE: So she's called Kallmorgen.

FRAU WINTER: I shall be back between ten and eleven.

GOLDSCHMIDT: You will look to see if we're still here.

FRAU WINTER: I think it's unlikely that before midnight —

GOLDSCHMIDT: Who knows?

FRAU WINTER: As usual — you don't stir from here, but get ready. No luggage, only your coats and a bag.

GOLDSCHMIDT: Is it a dark night?

FRAU WINTER: Moderately. Waning moon, last quarter.

GABRIELE: Wonderful! A walk by night.

FRAU WINTER: About twenty minutes' walk.

GABRIELE: Is that all!

FRAU WINTER: And even that not certain. Perhaps Frau Kallmorgen won't agree. And I can't think of anyone else. You must try to think of some other way, just in case. And I shall rack my brains too, on my way there.

GOLDSCHMIDT: And perhaps on your way back too.

GABRIELE: Kallmorgen hasn't a bad sound. Rather a hopeful one, in fact.

FRAU WINTER: I'll just quickly do the washing-up, my best ideas come to me when I'm washing up. No, let me do it by myself, Gabriele. *(Goes out.)*

GABRIELE: You must think, she said. I should rather have washed up, and sung praises to the day as I did it. It would have rounded it off nicely for me.

GOLDSCHMIDT: Not before midnight.

GABRIELE: Yet it began well, this day.

GOLDSCHMIDT: Did it begin well?

GABRIELE: I thought so this morning. One of those days one keeps ahead of — do you know what I mean, Grandfather? Even when you put on your shoes a streak of water between you and the shoes, a radiance.

GOLDSCHMIDT: Let's keep ahead of it then.

GABRIELE: That's not difficult, today.

GOLDSCHMIDT: But I have a feeling that it would be worthwhile.

GABRIELE: In that case shouldn't we leave now? Quietly open the door to the passage, carry our shoes in our hands and leave the washing-up and the illustrated weekly behind?

GOLDSCHMIDT: Where to?

GABRIELE: You don't like the idea of my forests. What about the canal?

GOLDSCHMIDT: That remains as a last resort.

GABRIELE: You suggest something.

GOLDSCHMIDT: What do you say to — our story?

GABRIELE: You're clinging to the illustrated papers, Grandfather. With a game of halma and a duet to follow —

GOLDSCHMIDT: No halma and no illustrated papers. No possibility of escape, no picture, no report; no, the story itself!

GABRIELE: Story-telling indeed. An hour ago it still made sense; but now?

GOLDSCHMIDT: *(hesitantly)* As a matter of fact; only now.

GABRIELE: The girls have been found. What more can we add?

GOLDSCHMIDT: We've already admitted the mistake in calculation.

GABRIELE: So they won't be found. That's all right too.

GOLDSCHMIDT: I don't know whether they'll be found or not.

GABRIELE: No, we don't know. Only Frau Kallmorgen knows.

GOLDSCHMIDT: Let's start again. The equation has not been solved.

GABRIELE: We go to a great deal of trouble, and in the end the answer is nought.

GOLDSCHMIDT: Try it.

GABRIELE: You try it. We're both the same age.

GOLDSCHMIDT: But your sight is better. I can't see the wood for the trees any more.

GABRIELE: No friendly wood, no friendly trees, but a child's forest full of terror, with brigands in the brushwood. The story wants a contribution from me.

GOLDSCHMIDT: Perhaps we'll find it. Perhaps there are raspberry canes hidden in that wood.

GABRIELE: Sloes, Grandfather. But come on, if you want to see for yourself. Let me take your hand in mine, my aged hand.

6

LENA: Signor Bottari, wouldn't it be better for us to separate?

BOTTARI: One course is as good as another.

BIANCA: Or as bad.

LENA: Perhaps then they'd at least find some of us.

BOTTARI: Perhaps then they would never find some of us.

MARIA: I feel as though we've been here a whole eternity.

ANTONIA: You forget that we've moved five times.

BOTTARI: True. And which place was better?

LENA: If this place were especially good, they would have found us.

BOTTARI: Perhaps they're on their way to this place. And if we went somewhere else we shouldn't be found.

LENA: Or the other way about.

BOTTARI: That may be too.

BIANCA: Leave it to Signor Bottari, Lena; he'll decide.

LENA: But he doesn't decide anything, and we just sit about here. Shouldn't we at least call out from time to time? *(She calls out)* Halloh!

BOTTARI: Don't do that. Your throat will get dry.

LUCIA: And you'll get more thirsty.

BIANCA: Leave everything to Signor Bottari, Lena.

LENA: In that case we'll be here till we die of starvation.

BOTTARI: We're saving up our strength until they find us.

LENA: *(mockingly)* Until they find us. But I want to be found sooner than that. I'm going. Who's coming with me?

MARIA: It's as though we were playing 'hide and seek.'

BIANCA: We'll be playing that too before long.

LUCIA: I'm staying here.

ANTONIA: So am I.

SEVERAL: I'm going. And so am I. I can't stand it here any longer. Let's all go!

BIANCA: Let Signor Bottari decide.

MARIA: What do you say, Signor Bottari?

(Silence.)

BOTTARI: I've already said that I consider it wiser to stay here.

LENA: But you don't know any more than we do what course is the wiser.

BIANCA: Stay here, Lena.

LENA: We're going. Hold hands. Now *(further away)* lower your heads — to the right here. The passage gets lower.

BIANCA: Lena!

MARIA: Let her go, Bianca.

BIANCA: What about when we get home and Lena and the others are not with us. Signor Bottari, it will be dreadful.

ANTONIA: If we get home.

BIANCA: Can you still hear them?

MARIA: I can't hear anything.

BOTTARI: Who went off with Lena?

MARIA: Margarita, Clara, Anna —

BIANCA: Elvira.

MARIA: And four others.

BIANCA: You shouldn't have let them, Signor Bottari.

BOTTARI: Oh, do you think so?

ANTONIA: But Signor Bottari did let them.

BIANCA: I know he did, and I can't understand it.

ANTONIA: I understand it.

BIANCA: What do you mean by that?

MARIA: Yes, what do you mean by that?

LUCIA: *(more slowly)* What did you say, Antonia?

61

ANTONIA: Excuse me, Lucia, but I didn't say anything.

LUCIA: *(still slowly)* What you meant was, Signor Bottari let them go because it makes no difference whether we're here or elsewhere.

MARIA: What are you getting at, Lucia?

LUCIA: Because we're lost in any case.

MARIA: Lost!

BIANCA: Do you think Signor Bottari has given us up?

MARIA: Signor Bottari, say something.

BOTTARI: I have not given us up.

BIANCA: But if you hadn't given us up, Signor Bottari, would you have let Lena and the others go?

(Pause)

MARIA: Did you say something, Signor Bottari?

BOTTARI: I did not say anything.

BIANCA: Nothing at all? *(Silence)* But I'm sixteen years old! Surely it's absurd, almost ludicrous —

BOTTARI: What is?

BIANCA: The idea that I shall starve to death here. Just because of a little outing to Rome, just before the summer holidays —

MARIA: Do say something at last, Signor Bottari!

BOTTARI: I'm tired of your chatter. I can't bear to be asked the same question every three minutes.

BIANCA: What did I say!

BOTTARI: And to repeat the same answer every time: we shall not starve to death, we shall be found.

MARIA: That's just what we thought.

BIANCA: You no longer believe what you're saying, Signor Bottari.

MARIA: One can tell even from your voice.

BOTTARI: All right, then, in that case I've some hope that you'll give up asking these questions. My answer doesn't grow more convincing by being repeated incessantly. That's the case with all repetitions. That's all I wanted to say.

MARIA: So you do still believe —

BOTTARI: *(exasperated)* Yes, yes, yes.

BIANCA: You know as little about it as we do.

BOTTARI: I never claimed the contrary.

BIANCA: You're just as helpless.

BOTTARI: My hope is the same as yours.

MARIA: If I'd known that I should never have come with you. Naturally a girl thinks, if we've got him with us —

BIANCA: It's your fault, Signor Bottari. You led us astray.

BOTTARI: So it's come to that, after all.

LUCIA: It's not Signor Bottari's fault.

ANTONIA: Be quiet, Lucia.

LUCIA: It's my fault. I was at the front of the line. I turned off into another passage on purpose.

BIANCA: What did you do?

LUCIA: I did it for a joke, that's all.

BIANCA: It was you?

LUCIA: Yes, me.

MARIA: I haven't taken it in yet. Do you mean to say it's because of you that we're here, Lucia. Because of a joke?

LUCIA: Yes.

(Silence)

MARIA: In that case I'm going to kill you. Do you hear?

BOTTARI: Nonsense, Maria.

MARIA: I've got a fine heavy stone just next to me — that will do. I'm going to kill you.

ANTONIA: *(laughs)*

MARIA: *(beside herself)* Pick up stones, all of you!

BOTTARI: Hold her back.

LUCIA: Leave her. Come on, then, Maria, go ahead and kill me.

ANTONIA: Ridiculous. We're all going to die in any case.

(Silence.)

BIANCA: Who said that?

ANTONIA: I did, Antonia.

BIANCA: It was definite enough, anyway. Not like Signor Bottari

LUCIA: *(in despair)* You'll never be able to accept it, that I just turned off like that to die!

MARIA: Lucia Torrini, a girl I would never have truck with, a girl in my form of whom I never took any notice. No, not even fate, but Lucia. *(With an effort, breathlessly)* As long as I have breath enough to say it, I shall tell you that it's your fault.

ANTONIA: You're just being stupid, Maria.

LUCIA: Let her say it.

MARIA: At least I know now why I'm still breathing this dank air, and what I'm breathing it for; it's your fault, Lucia, it's your fault! Lucia Torrini, the third desk from the last in the middle row —

LUCIA: Forgive me!

BIANCA: Useless bickering! I'm going to go and join Lena and the others, and I don't care whose fault it was.

ANTONIA: Bianca, don't go.

BIANCA: Even if I have to crawl on all fours: I want to get out of here, I want to get to the light, I want to get back to Viterbo. I want to live. *(She calls out)* Lena, Lena!

ANTONIA: They can't possibly hear you now.

MARIA: *(more calmly)* You're right, Bianca. Let's go. Even if we die; at least it won't be with those whose fault it is. Come on! Come on, all of you!

LUCIA: Forgive me first!

BIANCA: What difference does it make to you or me? I forgive you.

LUCIA: Say that you forgive me, Maria.

MARIA: I shall always say that it's your fault. As long as I can speak at all. *(She calls out)* Lena, where are you? Bianca, Sofia!
(The sound of several footsteps moving away, stumbling, faltering. The calls subside.)

BOTTARI: Anyone still here?

ANTONIA: Me, Antonia.

LUCIA: Lucia.

BOTTARI: Anyone else?
(Silence.)

LUCIA: No one else.

BOTTARI: All right. Three of us.

LUCIA: All right?

BOTTARI: We've been counted, that's reassuring. Or do you want to follow them?

ANTONIA: No.

LUCIA: No.

BOTTARI: That worries me.

ANTONIA: Why?

BOTTARI: There's no hope for me, anyway. But for you?

ANTONIA: Hope or no hope. If we're going to be found, we don't know where. So we stay here. The argument is logical.

LUCIA: We'll save our strength. You tell him, Antonia. I'm afraid Signor Bottari no longer knows his own wisdom.

BOTTARI: It's nice to hear you say that. But I should say cunning, and I don't know my own cunning well enough. What if we are not found?

ANTONIA: Then it makes no difference anyway.

LUCIA: So we'll stay.

BOTTARI: Is that still wise? I expected more of you. *(Hesitantly)* In a situation like ours one relies not on one's head, but on one's feet.

ANTONIA: We have our reasons. Mine are romantic.

LUCIA: As for mine, they're obvious.

BOTTARI: But you haven't yet given up hope, have you?

ANTONIA: I wish I knew. I don't know my own mind. *(After a while)* Is that how it has to be — hope or despair?

BOTTARI: That's the rule. The rest is beyond my competence as a teacher.

ANTONIA: It is so hard, then, to break with the old syllabus.

LUCIA: It's easier for us, because we never even knew it. For us, the next maths lesson could always be the final revelation.

ANTONIA: *(contemptuously)* The middle school test to qualify you for a middling life.

BOTTARI: Not so arrogant!

ANTONIA: And what if this were the next lesson? The extraordinary the utterly ordinary?

BOTTARI: Not in the syllabus.

ANTONIA: I mean, so that it wouldn't be worth making a great to-do about it. The period of darkness. Just ordinary. At best: voluntary attendance, afternoon lesson, an empty school building, in heaven by the evening.

BOTTARI: Didn't you come last in your class, Antonia?

ANTONIA: Second from last.

BOTTARI: Then leave me the place behind you. I'm a bad pupil. My only hope is that indifference will come of itself. Then I could still catch up with the aims of the class, by doing nothing, by sitting still.

7

GOLDSCHMIDT: Indifference, Gabriele?

GABRIELE: Can you suggest anything better?

GOLDSCHMIDT: Your Signor Bottari thinks that it comes of itself like sleep. That's a standpoint on which you can also sit.

GABRIELE: *(laughs)* An attitude that comes of my laziness, my passion for easy chairs.

GOLDSCHMIDT: But who's enough of an acrobat to walk to the easy chair on which he's already sitting?

GABRIELE: *(weary)* It all depends on your metaphors.

GOLDSCHMIDT: Yes, perhaps.

GABRIELE: Or on the prospect called Kallmorgen — that doesn't call for any wise saying. It's nearly ten.

GOLDSCHMIDT: 'The night advances.' The surprise is what I'm waiting for. Down there in the catacombs.

GABRIELE: They're all asleep. They've managed it.

GOLDSCHMIDT: We need something different from sleep.

GABRIELE: What's the use of this game?

GOLDSCHMIDT: This game? Don't grudge ageing people their sleep, and their bridge and their football.

GABRIELE: *(close to tears)* But I want to grow old. And I *shall* grow old. Frau Winter is on her way. She's hurrying, she's walking hurriedly, she's talking hurriedly, Frau Kallmorgen is listening hurriedly. They'll reach us yet. That's all I know. What do you want?

GOLDSCHMIDT: I want *you* to find us, before — before *we are* found, perhaps.

GABRIELE: That's more than I know.

GOLDSCHMIDT: It certainly is.

GABRIELE: Frau Kallmorgen, a lady with white hair, and kindness itself. Frau Kallmorgen, oh, I'm hanging on to that name as to a rope. Grandfather! no, not even that now — no form of address, no relationship. What shall I call you?

GOLDSCHMIDT: You see? On the way to becoming what one is. Outlines in invisible ink, a childish game, fire makes them visible. A house, a face, possibilities of good fortune.

GABRIELE: Possibilities, outlines. In one word: misfortune, Grandfather.

GOLDSCHMIDT: One word is not enough.

GABRIELE: Quiet!

GOLDSCHMIDT: Well?

GABRIELE: It's nothing. Only our conversation made me listen. I suddenly thought —

GOLDSCHMIDT: Now I can hear it. Footsteps. Frau Winter.

GABRIELE: Frau Kallmorgen. No. There's no such name, she's a fiction. *(she laughs)*

GOLDSCHMIDT: And it's boots, too, Gabriele.

GABRIELE: Is it?

(They listen. A ring on the bell.)

GOLDSCHMIDT: *(calmly)* You're right. Frau Kallmorgen is a fiction, she no longer exists. But the catacombs? Quick. What does Antonia say? *(A louder ring on the bell.)*

8

ANTONIA: Who's calling me?

BOTTARI: No one's calling.

ANTONIA: I heard a signal.

LUCIA: Quiet!

BOTTARI: Nothing.

ANTONIA: Perhaps it was only for me. Our front door bell, when there are visitors; the voices of my parents welcoming the visitors.

LUCIA: Voices, Antonia? That's a bad sign.

ANTONIA: The moment before they call you in.

LUCIA: Don't forget that your dreams will leave you. They come as near as that just before they vanish.

ANTONIA: Yes.

LUCIA: My ears are less sharp. All I can hear is the silence digging in its claws.

ANTONIA: *(as though to herself)* Rescue. Not water now, not lamps and not bread. Nor dreams either, nor voices. Only rescue, unalloyed. *(After a pause, more vigorously)* The other side of the moon, the one we have never seen. That's where I want to live.

BOTTARI: *(mockingly)* Happy landing.

ANTONIA: I should have liked to take you with me, Signor Bottari.

BOTTARI: Me?

ANTONIA: You and Lucia and the whole class.

BOTTARI: Oh, thanks very much. But I prefer to depend on my five senses, on our feeble hopes.

LUCIA: And I on my anger, which still keeps me warm. The other side of the moon? No, Antonia, it's no brighter there than here.

ANTONIA: Darker, dark enough at last. It gleams. I feel as though everything that happened in my life only pointed to this, the school exercises and the nursery rhymes, as though they all pointed to this moment, the moment of my acquiescence.

LUCIA: Don't forget that we're going to die of hunger, Antonia, and thirst, that we're going to cling to this floor like flies to their last wall — and you too.

ANTONIA: I've no advantage over you but my courage and, because of

67

it, a kind of happiness. *(After a while)* I remember that everybody prayed, as long as there was still hope that we'd be found.

BOTTARI: It was as pointless then as it is now.

ANTONIA: I think one can only pray when one has ceased to want anything from God.

BOTTARI: *(angry)* Well, pray, then!

ANTONIA: Yes, God, yes, yes, yes.

9

(The bell rings.)

GOLDSCHMIDT: Before midnight after all.

GABRIELE: Yes.

GOLDSCHMIDT: Perhaps they'll go.

GABRIELE: Yes, perhaps.

GOLDSCHMIDT: And perhaps it's Frau Winter anyway, perhaps she forgot her latchkey.

GABRIELE: *(almost gaily)* Or Frau Kallmorgen, coming without a latchkey.

(Picking the lock.)

GABRIELE: Do you hear them?

GOLDSCHMIDT: *(calmly)* They're forcing the lock.

GABRIELE: That wasn't the rule till now. A pity that we're exceptions.

GOLDSCHMIDT: Don't worry, we're not.

GABRIELE: *(mockingly)* Not to stir from here, that's what Frau Winter said.

GOLDSCHMIDT: Get ready, Gabriele.

GABRIELE: Don't worry, I am ready.

(Footsteps drawing closer. The door is flung open.)

GOLDSCHMIDT: That's right, we're here.

(Footsteps.)

THE YEAR LACERTIS

VOICES, PAUL, LAPARTE, BAYARD, KINGSLEY, ZEEMANS, RICHARDS, OLIVEIRA, MANUELA, THE OTHER MANUELA

PAUL: The palm trees in front of the alms-house form a dense grille, bringing human footsteps, like time, to a stop. Is it twenty years ago, or thirty? Perhaps I could work it out if I made the effort the crosses on the burial mound would help, even where the inscriptions have been washed away by the rain or covered by the rank creepers. What has time become? The colour of a briar rose and the glitter of a snakeskin.

So I don't even know the number of the year that preceded it all. Perhaps it was 1880, but in my recollections I have called it Lacertis, a word that had meaning for me at that time although it makes no sense and I knew that it wasn't the right word.

I heard the right word on New Year's night of that same year, and I heard it in my sleep.

I was lying in a ground-floor room and the window was not quite shut behind the curtains. The sound of drunks walking home and the striking of the clock on St Paul's penetrated my dream. It was shortly after six.

I started when I heard the word. Someone who was passing my window must have spoken it, in conversation and by the way, though it was the word that unravelled all mysteries. While it rang out the world was transformed and comprehended, but it was no sooner uttered than forgotten. I leapt out of bed and rushed to the window. A man and a woman were walking towards the main street. Both wore black coats, the man a silk hat, the woman, who was almost as tall, something small and fashionable. It seemed that both were a bit unsteady. Were they laughing too? I called out, but they didn't turn their heads and disappeared round the corner of Fisher Street. I dressed as fast as I could and ran out in the hope of catching up with them.

Thick snowflakes fell on their tracks, which I soon lost. I had possessed the philosophers' stone for one lightning flash. Can one find it a second time, when even the first time all search is in vain? Chance was my only hope.

I did not meet those two; nor even two others like them. In fact it seemed that the streets were being deserted, and when the ringing of a horsedrawn tram had subsided in the distance, I was left to my own devices in a stony moonlit landscape, veiled in the snow that drifted icily from outer space against the dockside warehouses.

Only special landmarks gave me a clue to my whereabouts. The angel who keeps his torch lowered over the names of the fallen emerged from the gloom. For a moment it seemed comforting to me that my brother's name was among those on the memorial tablet, and that probably, therefore, he was one of those who knew the word and had no need to run about in the snow to look for it.

There was the low wall that usually gave one a view of the port. That day there was something unusual about it. Had someone put down his baggage, a half-filled kitbag, and left it there for the snow to settle on? Or had they set up a piece of sculpture there to flatter the townspeople's artistic sense in sun and snow? I went closer and saw a man crouching on the parapet half covered with snow like an abandoned kitbag or like a stone figure that endures every kind of weather.

In the open air.
PAUL: A fine hour to sit about with no roof over your head.
LAPARTE: Who would find me if I stayed at home?
PAUL: Did you want to be found? Well, I've found you. Even though I was looking for something different.
LAPARTE: Tonight there's nothing better to be sought or found than me.
PAUL: That sounds promising.
LAPARTE: Would you like to touch my hump?
PAUL: What for?
LAPARTE: They say it's lucky. Remember, this is the first night of the year. Luckier than a horseshoe, a four-leaved clover, or a chimney-sweep. Enough luck for the whole year, and you can have it for a silver dollar.
PAUL: More than I can afford.
LAPARTE: Half a dollar then, as it's nearly morning.
PAUL: I should feel I was getting it too cheap. Is there no fixed price?
LAPARTE: You are ignorant, but —

70

PAUL: Well?

LAPARTE: But have it in you to become one of those who know. Here's my hump.

PAUL: You're frozen.

LAPARTE: That doesn't astonish me.

PAUL: Come back with me and warm yourself. I'll make some tea.

LAPARTE: But what if another should come, in need of luck?

PAUL: Drunks are happy, and the night is over. No one will come now. Does it work when the night is over?

LAPARTE: Not so well.

PAUL: Come on, then.

Room

PAUL: Punch would have warmed you even better. But I thought that maybe you'd had enough of New Year's night.

LAPARTE: What about you?

PAUL: I drank till two o'clock in the morning. Grog, punch and wine.

LAPARTE: Are you a painter?

PAUL: As you see.

LAPARTE: Very true to life.

PAUL: Feeling warmer already?

LAPARTE: The jackdaw there, the lapwing. And what about that one over there, the unfinished one? Can't make much of it yet.

PAUL: A fox coming out of the wood. I often paint it, always the same way. A popular prize for rifle-club competitions.

LAPARTE: Very neat piece of work, I must say. So's that gecko over there.

PAUL: You're quite an expert. Will you have a biscuit?

LAPARTE: Thanks.

PAUL: Early on New Year's Day biscuits are best.

LAPARTE: Do you paint other things too, portraits, historical scenes?

PAUL: No.

LAPARTE: Only animals?

PAUL: Only animals.

LAPARTE: Excellent.

PAUL: Why should it be excellent?

LAPARTE: It seemed so to me.

PAUL: Let me fill your cup.

LAPARTE: I feel much warmer now. I shall be going soon.

PAUL: Did I seem churlish? I find my paintings abominable.

71

LAPARTE: I don't know anything about paintings, but I do know about animals. That's why I said they were good.

PAUL: And it could be that I was churlish because it wasn't you I was looking for.

LAPARTE: Who then?

PAUL: Let's say a man with a silk hat and a lady with a jaunty toque.

LAPARTE: A pity it's me, so that it may seem presumptuous of me to say ...

PAUL: Go on, say it.

LAPARTE: What a man finds is what he's been looking for.

PAUL: What I was looking for was a word.

LAPARTE: A word?

PAUL: A particular word.

LAPARTE: Out in the street?

PAUL: Why not? Wait a minute. I'm close to it now. There must have been an A very near the beginning — at least I think so. But it's easy to be mistaken.

LAPARTE: A word you've heard?

PAUL: Not *a* word, the word. The only word.

LAPARTE: In that case there's no A in it.

PAUL: I think there is. It could have been Greek or Latin.

LAPARTE: Really?

PAUL: It sounded like — yes, like 'Lacertis'.

LAPARTE: Lacertis?

PAUL: No, that's not it.

(LAPARTE *laughs*.)

But it could have been something like it.

LAPARTE: Something like!

PAUL: That's the nearest I can get. Lacertis! Yes, it was almost that.

LAPARTE: Almost!

PAUL: Lacertis ...

LAPARTE: You've missed your chance. You won't find it now.

PAUL: You talk as though you knew.

LAPARTE: I know a great many words, just as far away from the real one as —

PAUL: Lacertis?

LAPARTE: Once uttered they fall on the ground like stones. Lacertis —

PAUL: Pretty meaningless, eh?

LAPARTE: It suggests lizards — Latin, *lacertus* — and must have something to do with reptiles.

PAUL *(meditatively)*: Lizards.

(LAPARTE *laughs.*)

Why do you laugh?

LAPARTE: I've written a book on lizards.

PAUL *(after a brief hesitation)*: That sounds implausible.

LAPARTE: A fad of mine.

PAUL: And I pick you up in the street after hearing that very word?

LAPARTE: That very word is what you didn't hear.

PAUL *(confused)*: So many coincidences.

LAPARTE: Too many, almost. The lizard, by the way, is connected with clairvoyance too. Consider Apollo —

PAUL: That, in turn, reminds me of last night. Would you call this a lizard by any chance?

LAPARTE *(mockingly)*: What, cast in lead?

PAUL: Manuela thought it was an archway.

LAPARTE: Manuela is probably right. Much more like an archway than a lizard.

PAUL: A pity; it would have fitted in so well. *(He laughs — they both laugh.)*

LAPARTE: Do you feel like coming to Brazil with me?

PAUL: A New Year joke?

LAPARTE: A scientific expedition. I could use someone who can paint lizards.

PAUL *(laughs)*: As accurately as I do?

LAPARTE: Half the expenses would be borne by the Belgian Academy of Science, the other half by me.

PAUL: By you? Out of the profit you made on New Year's Eve?

LAPARTE: Year after year I've wondered why everyone chose to invite me on New Year's Eve, when no one gives me a thought all the rest of the year — they way I've lived in Antwerp I might just as well have been in the Sahara or among the seals.

PAUL: It's Antwerp, then.

LAPARTE: Then I saw that it was my hump that made me so attractive. Ever since then I've left my home town at the New Year. I go to Paris or Amsterdam, London, Cologne or Hamburg. My hump is always welcome.

PAUL: For a silver dollar?

LAPARTE: One has to ask for money. Luck doesn't count if you get it for nothing.

PAUL: You didn't make me pay.

LAPARTE: Because you won't have any luck.

PAUL: You're very blunt.

LAPARTE: Come along to Brazil, then. You won't miss anything here.

PAUL: And over there?

LAPARTE: That lump of lead was wrongly interpreted. Not an archway but a ship. The one that goes to Pernambuco. A good omen.

PAUL: Didn't you say that I shan't have any luck?

LAPARTE: Think it over. I'll drop you a line. And I should be inclined to say: in many ways luck consists in having none.

PAUL: I took my strange guest to the station, where, in patched shoes, threadbare overcoat and hatless, he got on the train to Brussels and stretched out for the night on the red plush of a first-class carriage. Maybe he really was from Antwerp, maybe he really owned ocean-going ships? Nothing was impossible. As I walked home it occurred to me that I didn't even know his name. Did he know mine? Well, it didn't matter much; the thought of Brazil didn't fill me with irresistible longing. Back in my room the piece of lead still lay on the table. Was it a ship? I granted myself that 'archway' was the more convincing version. Then the thought struck me that only one night had passed since the lead had dropped with a hiss into cold water. Also, that on Manuela's account I might be reluctant to leave the town, and I recalled that she too had spoken of lizards, though in her story they'd had no real significance.

MANUELA: Our house was up on the hillside above the town and you could look across the bay to the rock of Gibraltar. A white, dazzling road led up to our house from the harbour. My favourite hiding-place was the hedge on our side of the low garden wall. There you had the best view of everything, and could see people right down below, very tiny, with very tiny carts and very tiny donkeys and very tiny boats, with red sails. Even the great ships in the harbour were tiny, and the still larger ones out at sea were even tinier. All this was so far away that often I was afraid we should be forgotten in our cool, white, tall house.

At times someone came up the road, and that was a comfort. I was thirteen or fourteen, and had a great craving for people. But I only dared to be close to them when I lay behind my hedge.

74

Otherwise I'd run away from them like a kid which a stranger tries to lure away from the nanny-goat. And yet I knew everyone likely to come that way: old Victoria, who delivered our meat and vegetables, the postman, the four labourers who worked in the half-disused quarry where the road came to an end. I still know the names of those four: Ramón, José, Ricardo, Carlos. How long since I last thought of them! But at that time they were like the four lines of a stanza, whenever they passed by in the morning: Ramón, José, Ricardo, Carlos; and at night, when they came down from the quarry, it was Ramón, Ricardo, Carlos, José. At night the order was always a bit different from what it was in the morning. What a good thing that the line could be shuffled round. The stanza always remained as beautiful as before.

Only once did a stranger come along. He came along at the hottest hour of the afternoon, and I saw him a long way off, appearing and vanishing again according to the bends in the road. He wore a peaked cap which he pushed back from time to time to wipe his forehead, and when he came closer I saw that he must be a sailor from one of the two boats that had docked last night in our harbour. Why was he coming up this way? It was a long and hot climb that led nowhere but to our house and the quarry.

By now I could have seen his face, but he kept his head lowered as he slowly mounted. He stopped near the wall and looked up to the hedge, and looked at the very place where I lay hidden. Though I was sure that he couldn't see me, I felt that I was being seen. But I remained there, crouching just as motionless as the lizard that was basking there on top of the wall.

For a few moments I saw the man clearly. He was obviously very young, with a fair but tanned complexion, thin lips and blue, very bright eyes. With those bright blue eyes he stared fixedly at my hiding-place, and it seemed as though he didn't blink once all that time. When he'd first raised his head, I hadn't known him, but after those few seconds he was familiar to me, I'd known him for a long time, he was like a brother with whom I'd grown up and I loved him.

Suddenly he swung round and went back the way he had come. My heart contracted, but it was natural that he should go. He went down the road, disappeared behind trees and rocks, emerged again and became smaller and smaller till he was one of those tiny creatures that swarmed about the harbour alleys, and till I no longer knew which of those creatures was he. He had come up all that way to look at the hedge behind which I was hiding; he had come to make himself known. That had been done, and there was no reason for him to stay longer.

PAUL: While I was recollecting the previous evening and Manuela in this way, I fell asleep at the table. Visible from far away and for a long time, a dazzling white sail cut into my sleep and it was also the resolve to look up Manuela.

When I awoke, however, this resolve seemed questionable to me. I made some tea and went back to my work on a picture which should really have been delivered by Christmas time. Perhaps it was better to run into Manuela again casually.

In the course of the next few days I finished the painting and started on a new one exactly like it for an art dealer at Ingolstadt. Having no real pretext for a visit, I decided that a letter was indicated.

I finished the second painting, and a third. Outside, it snowed. I rarely left the house.

Then I received a letter from a Mr Laparte in Antwerp. I was to come soon and make all the necessary arrangements. I quickly painted the last three orders for 'Fox breaking covert', sold my furniture, and one morning went to the station with a medium-sized suitcase. I had the impression that it had never stopped snowing in the mean time.

I spent three weeks at Laparte's house, where he lived alone with a large staff of servants. Then the ship sailed for Pernambuco.

In the open air. Ship's siren and sound of engines up and under.
PAUL: The ship to Pernambuco. I can't have got to Brazil any other way. But I search my memory for a ship and a long sea voyage. My memory has dismissed a great deal — things, I assume, for which it has no further use.

I start wondering uselessly what becomes of those things, where they settle, those homeless things. Perhaps the seagulls I must have heard are shrieking now in the dreams of a child, the captain's commands trouble the tender words of some lover, and the clatter of plates in the dining-room give comfort to some dying man. But what's become of the time, above all, of so much time that has passed since then? I'm afraid that it's being pieced together for a life that is good for nothing.

The ship to Pernambuco. But there's no one now whom I might ask how long the crossing took and at what ports we called. If forgetting is a sort of saving up, I don't doubt that there's also provision for an opportunity to spend all that accumulated capital.

I can see us all at Dr Bayard's house. I see his round grey beard and his dark eyes behind the pince-nez. He comes from Normandy and Laparte values him as an authority on snakes. He is the society doctor of Pernambuco. His sister keeps house for him, a shy old maid. I think she's either dumb or a phantom. There are times when her quietness is frightening.

The ship to Pernambuco. It has been broken up and its name forgotten in obsolete registers. There it is again, that suspicious word: forgotten. It insinuates itself everywhere. I shouldn't like to think that it is the little coin which I carried under my tongue and had to give the ferryman for my passage. After all, we were very gay at Dr Bayard's house, drank Brazilian red wine and real burgundy, and smoked black cigars. We must have spent a few weeks there. I learnt a bit of Portuguese, bought provisions, hired mulattoes, and did oil paintings of the snakes which Dr Bayard kept in glass cases. Laparte was the busiest of us all and made careful preparations for everything. The Indios were afraid of his deformity, and this gave him power over them. But I forgot to say that there were four of us. There was also Zeemans, and Kingsley. All wanted to collect something or other. Zeemans, beetles and flies, Kingsley, spearheads, cups and feather ornaments. It may be, too, that Kingsley collected beetles and Zeemans spearheads; I've forgotten, as I've forgotten the ship to Pernambuco. Sometimes I wonder whether it wasn't called Lacertis, since for some time the most unlikely thing has seemed the most plausible to me. For me that name would have a certain irony. For evidently the purpose of this lizard expedition was to show me that the word Lacertis could mean a great number of things as soon as one supposed that it meant anything at all.

As for what Dr Bayard said to me, at first I didn't take it very seriously. But my conversation with him has remained clear in my memory, more than anything else that we may have discussed at Pernambuco before leaving for the interior.

Room.

BAYARD: Mr Laparte wants to stay eighteen months?

PAUL: Roughly that.

BAYARD: And you can stay as long as you please?

PAUL: Yes.

BAYARD: What will you do when Mr Laparte has gone?

PAUL: I always do the same thing: I paint.

BAYARD: Do you think that you can live by painting in Brazil?

PAUL: In Brazil? I want to live in Europe.

BAYARD: Mr Laparte told me that you wouldn't be going back to Europe.

PAUL: You must have misunderstood him.

BAYARD: He told me that you've given up your flat and that there's nothing to keep you in Europe.

PAUL: Nor is there anything to keep me in Brazil.

BAYARD: I too arrived one day, with nothing to keep me here. That was forty years ago, and I've been here ever since.

PAUL: But why should I spend my life here?

BAYARD: I don't know you. Mr Laparte knows you better.

PAUL: I first met him three months ago.

BAYARD: And yet you've joined his expedition?

PAUL: Only because it happened that way. And really it all hinged on one word. Mr Laparte took it for a kind of portent, if you can use such big words about our acquaintance.

BAYARD: A word, you say. What word?

PAUL: It was Lacertis, and it reminded him of his lizards.

BAYARD: Lacertis?

PAUL: I overheard it one night.

BAYARD: Where?

PAUL: Through the open window. A couple of drunks. I guessed that it was of some significance for me.

BAYARD *(absent-mindedly)*: Of some significance for you.

PAUL: No doubt a groundless supposition. And it may not be the word I overheard.

BAYARD: It could have a different meaning.

PAUL: That's what Mr Laparte thinks too.

BAYARD: Lacertis. And just a shade different.

PAUL: There'd be quite a few shades to choose from.

BAYARD: I have grounds enough for distinguishing my shade from the others.

PAUL: Yours? What are its implications?

BAYARD: Laertes — that was your word.

PAUL: Would that make better sense?

BAYARD: The father of Odysseus.

PAUL: Those wanderings, Ithaca?

BAYARD: The wanderings *and* Ithaca.

PAUL: Significant for me, you'd say?

BAYARD: For me.

PAUL: For you?

BAYARD: Because I have a son.

PAUL *(laughs)*: Odysseus?

BAYARD: That's what I've called him at times in my own mind. But till now it wasn't clear to me that this would make me Laertes.

PAUL: It may be so. Perhaps my word *was* Laertes. It could have been Laertes, and could have been something quite different.

BAYARD: Laertes. That's the name which fits me.

PAUL: And you mean I heard it only for your sake? Only to bring it to you? Only to tell it to you as we stand here looking down at that empty, sun-drenched square?

BAYARD: Yes. Only for that.

PAUL *(laughs)*: And I suppose that now at last I know why I came to Pernambuco?

BAYARD: As we all know, Odysseus returned.

PAUL: None of us ever learnt a different version. If you want to trust Homer —

BAYARD: Homer and the drunken man in the night. To me too Odysseus will return, though he has travelled the seas for twelve years.

PAUL: We went up the Amazon in the paddle steamer and established our permanent quarters some hundreds of miles beyond Manaos. I was kept busy painting everything that Laparte caught; for he was afraid that few of the creatures would survive the voyage back to Europe, and wanted to bring them back as pictures at least. For Zeemans and Kingsley, too, I did some paintings. Happy days, when I sat in the shade in front of the hut, mixing colours. Naked, chattering Indian children surrounded me, and again and again they longed to taste those dabs of colour, just as our children long

79

for coloured sweets. It was hard to keep the tubes safe from them, for there might have been poisonous paints among them. Sometimes too there was no one standing about my easel, and then I heard their cries down by the river, where they were bathing, and perhaps there would be an ancient, pipe-smoking Indian woman, very ugly and as dirty as she was ugly, come to see my painting. Around dusk the smell of fish or game drifted out of the huts and the smell of maize bread and strong spices. Then the others came home from their fieldwork, we ate the meals which our native cook had prepared for us, and they commented on my paintings. They were severely critical if some mark on a reptile's back was not yellow enough or a red wasn't quite the natural shade. Before going to sleep they often complained of the moist heat. It didn't worry me at all, and in those sultry nights I slept under my mosquito net as though I'd never known anything different.

Happy days — I don't know whether they amounted to weeks or months. One evening, as we sat eating, they ended; without my noticing, Laparte's words put an end to them.

Half-open room.

LAPARTE: I got them to paddle me to a new place today. I had the feeling that this locality is exhausted for my purposes. What about you?

ZEEMANS: It's all the same to me. I can find the things anywhere as many as I need.

KINGSLEY: A change would be better for me.

LAPARTE: By the way, I hear that there's a white man three days' journey from here, with another tribe.

ZEEMANS: Who'd be useful to us?

LAPARTE: Who is lying ill there.

PAUL: Since when?

LAPARTE: I couldn't discover the precise circumstances.

ZEEMANS: Malaria, I suppose.

LAPARTE: I don't know. It was all a bit vague.

KINGSLEY *(yawns)*: Someone ought to look into it some time.

PAUL: I wonder why the Indians don't move him on.

KINGSLEY: Or why they haven't done him in, you might also wonder.

ZEEMANS: Yes, there are all sorts of questions one could ask.

PAUL: It would be best to ask him.

LAPARTE: That's what I thought. One of us should go there. Drugs, some

80

tea, a blanket —

ZEEMANS: Very thoughtful of you.

KINGSLEY: That reduces all the questions to one.

LAPARTE: Who's going?

ZEEMANS: I'm rather behind with the cataloguing.

KINGSLEY: There's no need for me to explain why I can't get away at this moment.

PAUL: You seem to be looking at me, Mr Laparte.

LAPARTE: Only because I'm waiting to hear your reason for not going.

ZEEMANS: But perhaps it would matter least to you ...

KINGSLEY: Whether you do your painting here or take a little trip up the river.

ZEEMANS: Bound to find some good subjects on the way.

KINGSLEY: Yes, and a change of company at last.

PAUL: The hut in which Richards lay ill was in bad condition. It was evening, and through the chinks in the wall light penetrated and formed a barrier between him and me. He lay in one corner on a bed of dry leaves. A bowl and a jug were beside him, and that was all. As I entered he propped himself up and turned his face towards me; or rather turned what had once been his face.

In the hut.

RICHARDS: Please get out.

PAUL: We heard about you and thought we might be able to help in some way.

RICHARDS: There's nothing I need.

PAUL: Is it malaria?

RICHARDS: It's leprosy. That's why I advise you to leave.

PAUL: Oh, it can't be all that infectious.

RICHARDS: One could even say, not infectious at all.

PAUL: Why should I go, then?

RICHARDS: I don't much like being looked at.

PAUL: There are things one could do for you. You're not lying comfortably.

RICHARDS: Insecticide, disinfectant, bars on the window, barbed wire about the place. I've heard enough about all those things. I want to die the way it suits me.

PAUL: You won't be doing that just yet.

81

RICHARDS: I've paid for it with filth and vermin; it's a simple account.

PAUL: Who brings you food and drink?

RICHARDS: The Indians. They help me out of fear.

PAUL: I'm afraid too, I could help you too.

RICHARDS: Go, I tell you; the others went.

PAUL: What others?

RICHARDS: I've thought of something I could do with.

PAUL: What is it? Maybe —

RICHARDS: Whisky.

PAUL: Do you think it would be good for you?

RICHARDS: That isn't the point.

PAUL: Who were the others?

RICHARDS: Nor is that — now. Have you brought any whisky?

PAUL: There's some back at our camp. A few days' journey from here.

RICHARDS: Will you fetch it?

PAUL: Yes.

RICHARDS: There were four of us. When they realized what it was, they cleared out. I've been here a year. *(With animation)* Really whisky wouldn't be at all a bad thing. But I don't believe you'll come back.

PAUL: Wait and see.

RICHARDS: Besides, I'd rather you didn't come back than have you treat me as a sort of poor Lazarus.

PAUL: Did you say Lazarus?

RICHARDS: There's a kind of pity, you know —

PAUL: What made you think of Lazarus?

RICHARDS: How could I fail to think of him?

PAUL: It reminds you of Lacertis, doesn't it?

RICHARDS: Of what?

PAUL: Perhaps it won't be me, after all, who brings you the whisky. There are four of us. I shall have to consult the others.

RICHARDS: The others — they're the ones a man should distrust.

PAUL: I should be happier if Lacertis were connected only with lizards.

RICHARDS: When I look at you, I can well imagine your staying here in my place, even without having leprosy. *(He laughs.)*

PAUL: Aren't you presuming rather?

RICHARDS: It's the small presumption of those who take a long time to die. Of course, it's no less irritating for that. But please don't think that I'm complaining. It's a pleasant disease which doesn't hurt. One grows insensitive. What more can one ask?

82

PAUL: I was full of resentment against Richards, much as I pitied him. To be left to rot alive, abandoned by everyone, was that a good reason for being presumptuous? Were people fools just because they weren't sick? Let the others get his whisky! I'd gone on the first trip. The second wasn't my business.

In the open air

PAUL: Not infectious, he says.

ZEEMANS: I hope you took the necessary precautions all the same.

LAPARTE: Some Lysol in the water when you wash.

ZEEMANS: That's not enough.

PAUL: Look, if you're worried —

LAPARTE: Don't let us quarrel now, please.

KINGSLEY: Infectious or not, there's precious little we can do for the fellow.

ZEEMANS: Poor devil.

KINGSLEY: Where are you off to?

ZEEMANS: I'm turning in. Had a hard day.

LAPARTE: I wish you a good night, Zeemans.

PAUL: Have we had easy days?

KINGSLEY: No. Or yes. In any case, let's try to make the next ones easier.

PAUL: That's no problem. Apart from Richards.

LAPARTE: So it's whisky he wants.

KINGSLEY: Have we got enough?

PAUL: He's ill.

KINGSLEY: And whisky will do him more harm than good.

LAPARTE: I'm not so sure.

PAUL: I'm quite sure that it will make no difference to his state of health.

KINGSLEY *(decisively)*: I propose that we take him to the coast. There's sure to be an institution somewhere for such cases. That's where he belongs.

LAPARTE: This possibility has one advantage: it would look as though we'd done something for the man.

KINGSLEY: Well?

LAPARTE: And at the same time it might look as though we'd done nothing for him.

KINGSLEY: Getting him there — is that nothing?

LAPARTE: All right then, let's take him to the coast.

PAUL: And pack up the expedition?

LAPARTE: How so?

PAUL: Didn't you say we'd take him down to the coast?

LAPARTE: One of us will do.

PAUL: The following morning Zeemans and Kingsley set out so early that I never saw them again. I packed what I needed for my second journey to Richards. Laparte joined me and watched me with his quick little eyes. I hated him at that moment.

Outside the hut

LAPARTE: A pity you're leaving us. So many days when you won't be painting, so many pictures the less for me.

PAUL: I ought to take my sea boots.

LAPARTE: If you consider the matter a little longer you'll discover that there's nothing you should not take.

PAUL: You're right. I'm packing too many things.

LAPARTE: On the contrary — too few. Are you going to leave your painting tackle?

PAUL: Do you think I'm going to have any time for painting?

LAPARTE: It will take you a week to get to Manaos, and three weeks to Para.

PAUL: How will he survive it? It's more like a journey from one graveyard to another.

LAPARTE: That's true of every journey — more or less.

PAUL: Or at best to a kind of prison.

LAPARTE: But among his own kind.

PAUL: Now don't talk about 'shared suffering'.

LAPARTE: I was just about to. Or should we not take him to the coast?

PAUL: I'm always the one who has to decide when both alternatives are equally bad. You people just turn round and go on collecting lizards or beetles.

LAPARTE: And you're the one to whom we leave human beings. In the Middle Ages, incidentally, lepers carried rattles which they had to use when they approached inhabited places. People threw them bread or money.

PAUL: I'm afraid of your learned digressions.

LAPARTE: They called them Lazarus rattles.

PAUL: Now don't try to tell me that Richards concerns me alone. I will take him some whisky, no more.

LAPARTE: No one is reproaching you.

PAUL: I shall take enough luggage for a few days.

LAPARTE: We shall be moving our headquarters within the next few days. It would be better for you to have all your things when you're looking for us.

PAUL: *All* my things?

LAPARTE: That's my advice.

PAUL: And what if I left some of them here?

LAPARTE: There would be a risk of theft.

PAUL: Or what if you took them?

LAPARTE: It always turns out that one's packed the wrong things.

PAUL: An answer to every question. But no more.

LAPARTE: And you'll bear in mind that money has been deposited in your name at Manaos, Para and Pernambuco. Don't forget.

PAUL: Lazarus. For days, while I was being paddled upstream the word obsessed me; I *thought* the word. I thought it with its three vowels and four consonants, and now I know that you can think a word. It moves, moves very fast and always straight ahead, an arrow shot from a bow — notched to the string it was once at rest, precariously, but still at rest. The marksman is unknown; and no one can be sure where the target is, or whether the arrow was shot senselessly into void and chance. To the right and to the left, above and below, images light up briefly, as in a lightning flash. They are too clear to last.

Lazarus, biblical garments, a stern hand that bars all accidents.

The sores, all the sores in the world, garish pictures out of medical textbooks, and we know what a horror the body is. What if we could see the soul in colour? The houses, agglomerations of houses, homesteads despairingly scattered over the landscape, horses, cows, flocks of sheep, all exerting themselves, but without avail. Libraries full of books, each a wordy concealment of loneliness. Roads which lead nowhere but back to our starting point. Prospects that please — as if we had any prospects.

Lazarus. Are there words that do not contain the world? A man lying in a hut in the jungle with leprosy. He waits for death. He is no worse off than anyone else. He is well enough. No need to bother with him. A few bottles of whisky, and off you go. A waste of good whisky. The idea that one should be concerned about

85

everyone, that's sentimentality. And the escape from it? Professional concern: midwives, nurses, doctors, priests, gravediggers, keeners, paid welfare workers of every kind — you should leave it to them.

And meanwhile, the suspicion, no, by now the certainty, that Richards was blind. Did he still have any eyes at all? Could I endure the sight of that face, which was no longer a face, for more than an hour?

Screams, shrieks from the bank. From the monkeys in the trees, or maybe parrots. Soon I shall wake up. But where shall I be lying then?

Lazarus, Lazarus.

In the hut

PAUL: No soda, you'll have to drink it neat. You'll feel as thirsty as the damned in Hell.

RICHARDS: I'm used to Hell.

PAUL: We think it our duty to take you to the coast.

RICHARDS: The devil take you as well!

PAUL: I can't force you.

RICHARDS: Whisky tasted better in my memory. But I shall get used to the taste again.

PAUL: There's hardly enough of it for you to get used to it again.

RICHARDS: You in a hurry to get away?

PAUL: No hurry, but —

RICHARDS: Put the bottle closer. How many have you got?

PAUL: Three.

RICHARDS: Three days, you might call it.

PAUL: A little more, perhaps.

RICHARDS: And what about you? Three days, three hours, or? *(When Paul does not reply)* Frightened? But it isn't easy to catch the thing. Catching leprosy is almost as hard as finding happiness. *(He laughs.)* You need to have a talent for it. Just think how few lepers there are.

PAUL: How did you catch it?

RICHARDS: I've been in too many ports and slept in too many beds to know for sure. It started five years ago. A few patches of red on the skin, on one thigh and on the belly, that was all. It went, and came back in different places. I paid no attention to it. But you don't want to listen to a case history. And really I know quite well how I caught it. I mean, what it was in me that made me catch it, that enabled me to catch it, if you like.

PAUL: A predisposition, you suggested.

RICHARDS: I mean that point in the world where all things are decided.

PAUL: Is there such a point?

RICHARDS: I was on a Turkish ship at the time, and we'd called at Algeciras. There's no port quite so dead. And of course it isn't really a port, but a fishing village. Red wine is the only amenity. I complained about this to the landlord at the *fonda,* and he laughed and said Algeciras was the centre of the world, because everything stands still there and everything else revolves about it.

PAUL: Where's the centre of the world, did you say?

RICHARDS: At Algeciras. I don't think you're listening.

PAUL: Go on all the same.

RICHARDS: I went back on board, but next day for some reason we couldn't sail, and were bored again. By noon I couldn't stand any more of the local amusements. I strolled round the streets, and came to a road that wound up the hill. Walking up that hill in the heat wasn't exactly a pleasure; I wasn't going anywhere, but boredom drove me on. Suddenly I was at the centre of the world.

PAUL: At Algeciras.

RICHARDS: To be more precise, some way above Algeciras. The road made a bend there, there was a high wall and a hedge above it. A lizard sat on top of the wall, with its head raised, as though petrified half-way through some movement. But I had the feeling that a pair of eyes was gazing at me through the hedge, eyes which I couldn't see.

PAUL: Yes.

RICHARDS: Algeciras is near Gibraltar. You can look across to the rock.

PAUL: The road led up to a quarry.

RICHARDS: A quarry? Could be.

PAUL: But you didn't walk on.

RICHARDS: I didn't walk on. Have I told you the story before?

PAUL: No.

RICHARDS: I often tell it. To the tree-trunks and the water-jug.

PAUL: And after that!

RICHARDS *(confused)*: After that?

PAUL: A pair of eyes looked at you.

RICHARDS: Or the hedge itself.

PAUL: But you didn't hear anything? No sound, no word?

RICHARDS: Only the silence of Algeciras, around which the world revolved.

PAUL: And then?

RICHARDS: Then? No then. There was no then for me at that moment. And I couldn't stand it either. I turned on my heel and left, so that the lizard might run on and the eyes in the hedge might be those of a girl staring inquisitively at me as I went. In order that it might be so, I turned on my heel and left. Do you follow me? So that everything might be forgotten.

PAUL: I understand. But was everything forgotten?

RICHARDS: Algeciras was as before: the *fonda,* the port, the ship. And yet I tried in vain to see it as I'd seen it only an hour before. *(With more animation)* A familiar experience: you see a town for the first time. But then you live there for a long time, your view of it changes more and more, and you never see it again as you saw it in that first moment.

PAUL: Never again?

RICHARDS: Perhaps at times, as in a flash.

PAUL: But a flash of joy.

RICHARDS: When I walked down the hill I had spent many years in Algeciras. But there was something else. I never again saw anything anywhere as in that first moment. I knew everything, I had lived everywhere for a long time. And that's what leprosy really is. I caught it because I already had it.

PAUL: Is your sight still good?

RICHARDS: It's gradually going now. The worse I see, the newer everything becomes for me. I live backwards. Death — that's the moment when the world is as on the first day.

PAUL: The Indians who looked after Richards cleared a hut for me to live in during my stay. Richards was never fully awake for more than a few hours each day, spending the rest in a kind of coma. I had the feeling that he wasn't very far from that moment of which he'd spoken. The idea of taking him down to the coast became more and more absurd.

I had a good deal of time on my hands, and unpacked my painting gear. I didn't paint animals this time, I painted the hut in which Richards was to die, the path that led to it, and the jungle behind it. I thought I was painting this for Manuela. There was no need to tell her that death was part of the picture. It was a jungle landscape, nothing more. It was the best I ever painted, but bad enough all the same. Manuela never saw the picture. I suppose there are many things which concern me but which I never learn about, just as Manuela was never to know that painting. The whisky lasted longer than expected but on the sixth day it was finished. I considered the possibility of which no one had spoken; indeed, it seemed to me the most natural.

In the hut.
RICHARDS: You don't offer me anything today.
PAUL: The bottles are empty.
RICHARDS: And three days have passed?
PAUL: This is the sixth.
RICHARDS: You've stayed longer than you intended. Weren't you going to take me to the coast?
PAUL: You didn't want me to.
RICHARDS: You'll have to be going now, won't you?
PAUL: I'm staying.
RICHARDS: How long?
PAUL: I don't know.
RICHARDS: I know.
PAUL: I thought I'd stay as long as you want.
RICHARDS: When the time comes I shan't be wanting anything. You'll be bored. Would you light the candle, please?
PAUL: The candle?
RICHARDS: That's what I said.
PAUL: I've run out of candles.
RICHARDS: And now I see that it's broad daylight. The sun is shining on my hand. It's nearly time now, or I shall know darkness too long.

PAUL: On the tenth day a canoe arrived, to my surprise. The Indians drew me to the bank with their cries. There was Laparte, smaller and more hunchbacked than ever. In his white shirt he looked like a kitbag covered with snow, dumped indifferently and abandoned — just as he'd looked when I first set eyes on him. A harbour wall in winter, or the sun on the Amazon — the differences were slighter

than one might suppose, great at first, but cancelling themselves
out in time.

In the open air.
LAPARTE: I had the feeling that this was your 'at home' day, Paul.
PAUL: All my days have been so, recently. Anything in particular?
LAPARTE: Only my need for company and conversation.
PAUL: That house in front of us is mine.
LAPARTE: And Richards?
PAUL: Next door.
LAPARTE: He still — lives in it?
PAUL: Yes.
LAPARTE: Not a bad place.
PAUL: Not bad for what?
LAPARTE: To live in, of course.
PAUL: This way in. Take the folding chair.
LAPARTE: Ah, so you're painting again? New subjects?
PAUL: Only to occupy myself.
LAPARTE: You're short of lizards.
PAUL: If you say so.
LAPARTE: It's of your hut, isn't it? A memento.
PAUL: Richards' hut.
LAPARTE: A memento all the same.
PAUL: I suppose so.
LAPARTE: I'm surprised to find you still here. Shouldn't you have been
    on your way to the coast long ago? Wasn't that your plan?
PAUL: I'm staying a bit longer. That's to say, he's staying a bit longer.
LAPARTE: It comes to the same thing.
PAUL: The difference wouldn't be worth a quarrel.
LAPARTE: I haven't come here to quarrel. I wanted to ask you whether
    you'd come with me.
PAUL: No.
LAPARTE: Of course not. You'd already answered that question.
PAUL: Everything all right at base camp?
LAPARTE: Everything all right. I'm on my own there now.
PAUL: How so? Zeemans and Kingsley?
LAPARTE: If you recall, the northern tributary widens into a kind of lake
    after an hour's journey.
PAUL: You mean, the others have gone off by themselves?

LAPARTE: That route didn't suit me.

PAUL: But only a short time before you yourself had proposed —

LAPARTE: Second thoughts.

PAUL: A quarrel?

LAPARTE: Not a quarrel. Only Kingsley and Zeemans are annoyed, and rightly so.

PAUL: Why rightly?

LAPARTE: My decision to terminate the expedition as far as I was concerned took them rather by surprise.

PAUL: Me too.

LAPARTE: Irresponsibility is what Kingsley called it.

PAUL: And what are your plans now?

LAPARTE: My plans! *(He laughs.)* Yes, it's difficult to explain, I have no excuse to offer really. Except my hump. And no one will suffer financially.

PAUL: No one will attribute it to meanness.

LAPARTE: It may be the heat. Ten years ago it didn't matter to me. Now I can't sleep.

PAUL: That's how thoughts begin.

LAPARTE: And upset my plans. I begin to have doubts, every possible kind of doubt. Why lizards, for instance? Grown-up, serious people travelling for months, to catch lizards. It's absurd. And one turns and turns on one's bed, listening to the mosquitoes. One invents all sorts of reasons for lizards, and all are equally ridiculous. Amongst other things the thought occurred to me that I collected lizards only to bring you here.

PAUL: You think too much.

LAPARTE: One morning I get up and it's clear to me that I never want to see another lizard.

PAUL: And sleep too little.

LAPARTE: It's a fact that most people manage perfectly well without lizards.

PAUL: I'm not so sure.

LAPARTE: That was the day before yesterday.

PAUL: Too short a time for such decisions.

LAPARTE: I shall return to camp from here, pack up, and be on my way within a few hours. May I repeat my question, whether you would like to come —

PAUL: Certainly, your question has grown in weight.

91

LAPARTE: But your answer is the same? *(When Paul doesn't reply)* You don't need me any more. The picture, by the way, gets better and better. You've really brought it off this time. Altogether, it may be that you'll now find yourself turning to other subjects.

PAUL: The river flowed broad and muddy. As the canoe glided into the stream and gathered speed, Laparte raised one hand and waved to me. He was standing upright, but it looked as if he'd drawn his head even lower down between his shoulders and had sat down exhausted. He called out something to me, but I didn't catch it. It could have been the word which I had already once failed to understand. He had been here, and perhaps he knew it but didn't tell it to me. But it was possible, too, I thought, that it could only be told me when the speaker was so far off that I couldn't catch it. Distance is the prerequisite of happiness. I raised my hand and waved, although the canoe was no longer recognizable. At the same time I was raising my hand to wipe it all away — all the questions, the many possibilities, the leave-taking, Laparte, Zeemans. Farewell, the river flows broad and muddy, I shall go down that river myself and not return.

In the hut.
RICHARDS: You haven't been to see me all day. Did someone arrive?
PAUL: Yes, and we're in luck; he brought some whisky.
RICHARDS: The lizard man, was it?
PAUL: Two bottles.
RICHARDS: It may be enough.
PAUL: And tinned food.
RICHARDS: Excellent.
PAUL: Will you have a drop?
RICHARDS: Has he left again?
PAUL: He has.
RICHARDS: Where's he going? What will he do? No, that isn't what I want to know. It's something different. What will *you* do when you leave this place?
PAUL: Nothing special, I think.
RICHARDS: One doesn't really know for sure what is special and what isn't. It's special for me, because it will happen at a time when I'm no longer here. You'll be going to Manaos, but will there be such a

place as Manaos then? When for me it belongs to the delusions, you'll be walking through those wretched alleys past those cheap bazaars, past the counter of the ship's chandler, Minhos y Filho, and all these things put on a grave face though they no longer exist. Consider that, to the dead, it's the living who are phantoms. And yet you'll go on to Para and Pernambuco. Meanwhile all space will have been suspended, dissolved into something that isn't time either. The boulevards, the cafes, the evening walk, the newspapers, the coins in your purse — all goes on while the music of the spheres has begun to play. *(Laughing)* I'm good at consoling myself, don't you think? *(When Paul doesn't reply)* Then you'll cross the sea. And that, by the way, is something I can envisage even after I am dead. You'll cross the sea. But what will you really be doing?

PAUL: Looking for those eyes that stared at you through the hedge.

RICHARDS: Good God, you can't do the same as I did. Leave that to me — the only occupation that will then remain for me. You have time enough. Here's to a good journey. *(Slight pause.)* Well, won't you wish me the same?

PAUL: Here's to a good journey, Richards.

RICHARDS *(laughing)*: That's better.

PAUL: Richards died two weeks later. During most of that time he was unconscious and inarticulate. The Indians helped me to bury him. After taking whatever papers I could find in his kitbag, we burnt the hut and his few possessions. In the evening I read his papers and burnt them also.

That night I remained awake for a long time, listening to the night sounds. At times it was loud with animal life, then again one heard only the river, a monotonous roar which certainly would grow imperceptible one day to anyone who remained in this place. I regretted that there was no whisky left, only tobacco for my pipe. This lit up a small space in the hut. Outside there were the stars.

I thought of the monument on which my brother's name was inscribed, and thought of Richards, whom I had buried that day, like another brother. When I closed my eyes I saw the first night of that year in my mind, and the falling snow already blotting out the names. The flakes were quick as the night's thoughts.

How had I arrived here, at this one point of the world? Had

93

they all, had Manuela, Laparte, Richards, hadn't they all spoken the same word to me?

Towards dawn I fell asleep. I dreamed about Manuela.

Unreal.

PAUL: Here are the letters, Manuela.

MANUELA: So many of them! A whole coffin full.

PAUL: I've spent my whole life writing them.

MANUELA: When am I to read them all?

PAUL: They all contain the same thing. Only the stamps differ. This one is German, that one Belgian, that one Spanish.

MANUELA: Have you been to Spain?

PAUL: Near Gibraltar.

MANUELA: You haven't been to Spain. And those letters are not by you. There's nothing written in them. Empty envelopes.

PAUL: My life.

MANUELA: Other people's lives.

PAUL: All that wasn't me, then?

MANUELA: Not even an illness of your own.

PAUL: And I thought —

MANUELA: I thought so too, about myself. But those were different eyes with which I looked through the hedge. I must tell you something, Paul: the path does not lead to the quarry.

PAUL: I thought as much.

MANUELA: But you mustn't tell anyone.

PAUL: I must be off, Manuela. Can't you hear the ship's bells?

MANUELA: They're the bells of all the ships that have run aground.

PAUL: And the captain is a stickler.

MANUELA: Didn't you know, I'm coming with you? I've taken a holiday from work.

PAUL: It's only a small vessel. But if you come with us, there'll be room for all. Come on, then, quick!

PAUL: When I bathed in the river next morning I noticed several red patches on my right hip. Probably it was only that I'd lain in an awkward position during the night, and there was no reason yet to be anxious. By the time I arrived at Manaos — it took me about a week — the patches had gone again, but then suddenly I had them all over my body, and when I took the paddle steamer at Manaos,

I could no longer think of any good reasons for not being anxious.

It's a slow boat. Often it stops at places for no purpose that one can see, unless it were to entertain the alligators and parrots. The steamer approaches them with a loud ringing of bells, lies moored there for an hour or several, with not one human being to meet it; and then the wheels turn again and the boat moves on, while the ship's bell rings meaninglessly into the jungle.
(Departure of a paddle steamer, ship's bell. Sounds slowly fade out.)

In the open air.

PAUL: The bells of all the ships that have run aground. Laparte said I had no further need of him: how wrong he was! I need everyone. I need the groaning old men in the afternoon sun, the infants in their cradles, the child who can't do his homework, the woman knitting by the light of a paraffin lamp, the doctor who prescribed the wrong medicine, the drunken man who didn't feel cheerful. Whoever is afraid, needs them all. I fear for my life, though I am by no means certain about my illness.

Above all, I need Bayard. He'll tell me whether I've caught it, and if I have caught it, he'll know of a remedy made of snakes' venom and orchid juices. It's very comforting, Pernambuco, the sounds of the sea, Dr Bayard —

Room.

BAYARD: I thought you'd come. I've prepared everything and looked up the relevant literature. *(He titters.)*

PAUL: It appears that the relevant literature is amusing.

BAYARD: It's a rare disease, and one doesn't keep up with rare diseases as a matter of course. I've taken the precaution of examining Laparte also. So I'm in practice already.

PAUL: Laparte? Why, is he still here?

BAYARD: He was till the day before yesterday.

PAUL: I thought as much.

BAYARD: His boat sailed two hours after the funeral.

PAUL: What funeral?

BAYARD: Pretty red, those patches. Any pain?

PAUL: No.

BAYARD: My sister died suddenly.

PAUL: Your sister, did you say?

BAYARD: Oh, you hardly knew her. No point in involving your feelings. As for Laertes — *(Cuts himself short, tensely.)* You see, if I press my finger down here, the impression remains, and the skin doesn't grow taut again.

PAUL: Is that a bad sign?

BAYARD: Nothing is particularly bad.

PAUL: The skin does grow taut again, the impression does not remain.

BAYARD: You know better than I do.

PAUL: If I did, I shouldn't be here.

BAYARD: Just one more puncture, you'll hardly feel it.

PAUL: What were you going to say about Laertes?

BAYARD: That I was mistaken. How long have you had these patches?

PAUL: Five weeks.

BAYARD: I am not that Laertes, Odysseus will not return, this is no Ithaca. This is Pernambuco, a town with a harbour, docks, and a regular mail service. For instance you can receive a letter from Cape Town, and it will take a month at the most. And in it you may well read: Your son has died in the local prison. The date as well, needless to say. And a few official phrases draped around it. But the word 'died' remains legible beneath all the phrases and drapery. How's your appetite? Digestion all right?

PAUL: Doctor Bayard —

BAYARD: You're very sorry. I know. But I asked you —

PAUL: All quite normal.

BAYARD: And why does fate make this vulgar joke? Or rather, you? Why did you make it?

PAUL: I don't follow.

BAYARD: That's done. Your arm again, please. We've nearly finished. Suddenly one day my sister begins to talk madly, and a few days later she's vanished, and on a third day her corpse is found in the harbour pool. For my benefit, though, it was described as an accident.

PAUL: Where's the joke, Dr Bayard?

BAYARD: Can't you see it? Can't you see it yet? Laertes. Who induced me to put my trust in that name? Who called me Laertes?

PAUL: You did yourself.

BAYARD: The word came from you. And what we both forgot, there's another Laertes, not at Ithaca, but at Elsinore. His sister Ophelia,

96

who loved Prince Hamlet, went mad and drowned herself. A fine joke.

PAUL: A joke, you call it?

BAYARD: Laertes! My sister was fifty-nine, and if there was a Prince Hamlet in the case, he must have been bow-legged and bald. Laertes. Just a small confusion over the locality. Very funny, don't you think?

PAUL: Yes.

BAYARD: I must leave you for a moment now. Just a little test in my laboratory, I won't keep you long.

PAUL: I felt as though the jury were retiring for the verdict. Not guilty — attenuating circumstances. I sat on the wooden seat listening for footsteps, the creaking of corridors and the opening and shutting of doors. A long time passed before Dr Bayard returned. But I felt an upsurge of hope when I saw his face. He seemed satisfied.

Consulting room, as before.

PAUL: Well?

BAYARD: As far as your word is concerned, I can provide further variations on it.

PAUL: Touching my state of health?

BAYARD: In my mother tongue there's a word, *la certitude,* certainty.

PAUL: *La certitude.*

BAYARD: Doesn't it make you think of Lacertis? But what is one sure about, ever? *La certitude,* certainty — it's like an answer to which one doesn't know the question.

PAUL: Is everything all right?

BAYARD: Yes, everything is all right.

PAUL: That's all I wanted to know.

(A ring.)

BAYARD: Someone to see you, I should think.

PAUL: To see *me?*

BAYARD: Someone who wants to have a word with you.

PAUL: Apart from you, there's no one knows I'm here. Or is there?

BAYARD: Only two gentlemen.

PAUL: Acquaintances of yours?

BAYARD: I've never met them.

(Another ring.)
Wait. I'll open the door.
(He is heard to go out and speak to someone outside.)
The gentleman will be with you in a moment.
(He comes back.)
There are cases of leprosy that develop very fast, I mean develop fatally, a few weeks, or a few months. And there are others that drag themselves out over years, or even decades.

PAUL: That doesn't matter any more.

BAYARD: It continues to matter — always.

PAUL: I mean to me.

BAYARD: And one more thing: the Brazilian home for lepers used to be a monastery, occupied for a very long time by Italian monks. It is still called the Charterhouse, La Certosa.

PAUL: Your ingenuity is boundless, Dr Bayard.

BAYARD: Yes, it does remind you of Lacertis, doesn't it? No one could say that the word is quite meaningless.

PAUL: It certainly does remind me of it — irresistibly.

BAYARD: And you'll have a great deal more leisure to think about it, to acquaint yourself with the resemblances from the inside, as it were, once you've arrived there.

PAUL: Arrived where?

BAYARD: At the Certosa. The two gentlemen have come to fetch you. Everything is all right, monsieur — you have got leprosy.

PAUL: A two-wheeled cart, on which I lay like a bundle of rags. A mule at the shaft, sore with many beatings, as though it had leprosy too. Stubbornly it pulled us through the wide archway of the Certosa, reluctantly, and I knew that I had arrived. Half the size of a hand and cast in lead — hadn't the pillars and the arch lain on the plush cover of my table? At that time I hadn't known their meaning.

To the right and to the left of it the walls were covered with tall shrubs. Through all that growth one could see the pieces of glass at the top, green, brown and white. It was not a hospital that awaited me, but a prison. Whatever the crime, there was no doubt about the sentence.

The cells were inhabited by the disintegrating, the blind, by those cripples who crawled on all fours. Their tin plates were outside their doors as I was led through the passage; it was the hour when the beggars' soup was dispensed, and no sick person was allowed to leave his room. Doors were opened secretively behind us, disappointed eyes, disappointed groping hands. But all this didn't become clear to me till later, when I too waited hungry.

Not much more than this soup came to us from the outside world, unless one counted Dr Oliveira, our physician, who walked hurriedly through all those passages once a week, and the warders, who kept their distance whenever possible, were really guards, and carried truncheons. As for a priest, there was one among the inmates themselves, and the less serious cases served as gravediggers. Anyone who came to the Certosa was left to his own devices.

Soon the rainy season began. It began, and went on, and ended, a new summer began, a new rainy season, three years went by, and suddenly it seemed as though the clocks, which had long come to a stop, started to work once more. This happened when Manuela arrived, the other Manuela. Like me, she arrived when the empty plates were in the passages, and we opened the door and the soup still hadn't been ladled in. A broad mulatto woman in a garish green dress puffed and blew her way through the passage into the deaf-mutes' cell.

Manuela was very ill, so obviously ill that it was difficult to understand how she could have remained at liberty until that day. She had lived on garbage and slept under the arches of viaducts. Another beggar had reported her so that she wouldn't have to share her sleeping quarters with Manuela. To Manuela, the Charterhouse was paradise.

THE OTHER MANUELA: The soup isn't as bad as they all say. It's good, very good. There are little bits of meat in it.

PAUL: I like you, Manuela.

THE OTHER MANUELA: Oh Senhor, how can you like me? An old nigger woman with leprosy.

PAUL: I've got leprosy too.

THE OTHER MANUELA: I don't believe it. You're a good-looking man.

PAUL *(laughs)*: I like you, Manuela, because your name is Manuela.

THE OTHER MANUELA: Oh, that's a good reason. It's a beautiful name, don't you think?

PAUL: Mightn't all the Manuelas in the world be like one another?

99

THE OTHER MANUELA: If that's so, Senhor, tell me what the other is like. The one you're thinking of.

PAUL: Am I thinking of one?

THE OTHER MANUELA: I could do my best to be like her.

PAUL: No, you mustn't exert yourself.

THE OTHER MANUELA *(laughs)*: Well, confidentially: I am her. I am the other. You only need to forget my colour and my leprosy and a few little things besides. In short: forget me, and I shall be the other.

PAUL: Let's put it to the test, Manuela: where were you born?

THE OTHER MANUELA: I don't know.

PAUL: You're making it too easy for yourself. Do you know Algeciras?

THE OTHER MANUELA: The waiter in the Cafe Commercial?

PAUL: Algeciras is a town.

THE OTHER MANUELA: Now I remember. The town where I was born. Somewhere near Rio, isn't it?

PAUL: Wrong again, my dear. No, you don't know any of the names, Gibraltar, Antwerp, Laparte, Bayard —

THE OTHER MANUELA: Dr Bayard, do you mean?

PAUL: Do you know him, then?

THE OTHER MANUELA: Once I put my hand in a rubbish bin and a snake bit me.

PAUL: What then?

THE OTHER MANUELA: I went to see him, he hurt me, I don't like to think of Dr Bayard.

PAUL: He got me in here.

THE OTHER MANUELA: I'm not surprised; now he himself is in a house like a prison.

PAUL: What house?

THE OTHER MANUELA: A madhouse.

PAUL: Dr Bayard?

THE OTHER MANUELA: It must be two or three years ago that I went to see him. Soon after that it came out. There was a lot of talk about it in Pernambuco. They put him away when he set his snakes loose.

PAUL: A few years ago?

THE OTHER MANUELA: When I still had my looks; yes, a few years ago.

PAUL Next day Dr Oliveira paid his visit. After hurriedly going his rounds he retired to the porter's lodge, where he used to spend a few hours writing his reports.

I packed my case. There wasn't much to pack, a pair of shoes, three shirts, a pair of trousers, five handkerchiefs, four pairs of socks. That would do for a start. Laparte's money was still waiting for me at the bank. I hoped that a boat would be sailing soon. But even if all went badly I could still be in Europe within five weeks. I wondered how to approach Dr Oliveira and what to say to him.

A knock on a door.
OLIVEIRA *(inside)*: Who is it?
(Paul enters the room.)
You know that the sick are not admitted here.
PAUL: I'm not sick, Dr Oliveira, and even if I were I should come in.
OLIVEIRA *(coldly)*: I don't understand.
PAUL: Well, listen to me, then.
OLIVEIRA: What's the meaning of that suitcase?
PAUL: I've been here three years now.
OLIVEIRA: Not quite three years.
PAUL: The red patches I had at first disappeared after a few months.
OLIVEIRA: That doesn't mean anything.
PAUL: Since that time I've found nothing on me that would indicate leprosy.
OLIVEIRA: You've been here two years and seven months.
PAUL: And you've never once taken the trouble to examine me.
OLIVEIRA: You were examined by an expert.
PAUL: An expert in snakebites.
OLIVEIRA: With our equipment here we could never have arrived at such an exact diagnosis. You know that whoever has leprosy once will never be rid of it. Appearances are deceptive. There are cases that take a very long time to become acute.
PAUL: That may be, Dr Oliveira. But it isn't a medical discussion I want to have with you.
OLIVEIRA: What other kind of discussion, then?
PAUL: About experts and specialists. About Dr Bayard, who has spent the last three years —
OLIVEIRA *(quickly)*: Not when you were examined.
PAUL: Nor when he prescribed hot baths for snakebite. It's on the strength of a madman's report that I've been kept here for three years.
OLIVEIRA: I've already told you —

PAUL: Two years and seven months, and what I propose is that we leave it at that.

OLIVEIRA: Leave it at that?

PAUL: You'll make out a certificate for me, dated from today.

OLIVEIRA: That's blackmail.

PAUL: You may call it what you like. But do what I tell you — in your own interest.

OLIVEIRA: And is it in your interest too?

PAUL: I shouldn't make any claims.

OLIVEIRA: What do you want to get out for?

PAUL: I shall take the next boat.

OLIVEIRA: The next boat, of course. One always thinks that travelling will get one further.

PAUL: Everything has only begun.

OLIVEIRA: Be glad, then, that it's only just begun. Everything is much worse when it's drawing to an end.

PAUL: When it's drawing to an end. But it's going on. I'm well.

OLIVEIRA: Look around you in the world: how difficult it is for someone who hasn't got leprosy.

PAUL *(laughs)*: It's easy for you to talk.

OLIVEIRA: Everything becomes easy for the man who has found certainty.

PAUL: It was the wrong word that brought me here.

OLIVEIRA: This is the place you were able to reach.

PAUL: The wrong word, to the wrong place. I must look for the right one.

OLIVEIRA: You fool. Go ahead and travel, then, if you think you'll find it elsewhere. Here's your certificate.

PAUL: Goodbye, Dr Oliveira.

(The door opens and shuts.)

PAUL: Yes, that was the last word I would say to him. Goodbye, Dr Oliveira. It was all as simple as that. He wouldn't make many difficulties because he wouldn't dare. Then would come the wonderful moment when I walked out past the porter, and I would show him my certificate, and then there would be the palm grove and the view of the sea, and perhaps one might already see one of the ships —

I awoke from these daydreams into which I had fallen before my half-packed suitcase. I awoke with a sudden pain, it was like a knife-thrust that cut my dreams in half and slipped on into my heart.

It was the thought that none of the inmates must see me. I must creep out when I went to see Dr Oliveira, I must lay a finger on my lips when I passed the porter, and steal away in the cover of the shrubs.

But would that be the end of it? Even if I sailed off, in the boat, over the sea, to freedom — was not my only certainty the knowledge that I'd forsaken the others? Would I be sailing to freedom? Could there still be caresses without venom and words that gave me joy? I remembered that O'Connor was losing strength rapidly, and Juanita was pregnant, that in a few weeks' time we should be putting on our play, and that I'd promised Manuela to whitewash her cell for her. Professor Fervao was waiting for me to read him the seventh canto of the *Lusiads,* and something had to be done to amuse Jorge, whose wife had got a divorce. Feliz told me last night that Juanita's baby was his, and Maria wouldn't be capable of doing the washing-up much longer, as she had suddenly got worse. True, they could all die well enough without me, but I couldn't live without them.

Unreal.

OLIVEIRA: One always thinks that travelling will get one further. This is the place you were able to reach.

PAUL: Who had said that? No, not Dr Oliveira. Myself. Someone was calling me, a woman's voice, probably it was Manuela.

I unpacked the case again. There wasn't much to unpack, a pair of shoes, three shirts, a pair of trousers, five handkerchiefs, four pairs of socks — not much, but it was enough.

Then Manuela called me again. I went out to ask her what she wanted.

THE ROLLING SEA AT SETUBAL

VOICES:
PEDRO, *Catarina's servant*
FELIPE, *landlord of the inn*
OJAO, *servant of Camões*
LORD CHAMBERLAIN
CATARINA DE ATAIDE
ROSITA, *her maid*
LANDLORD'S WIFE
THE MOTHER OF CAMÕES

Rosita enters Dona Catarina's bedroom.
ROSITA: Your chocolate, Dona Catarina.
CATARINA: My chocolate. *(She stretches and sits up.)*
ROSITA: The tray on the coverlet, so that it touches her dressing-gown.
CATARINA: Carry out my orders, Rosita: don't repeat them like a parrot. Ten o'clock?
ROSITA: Exactly.
CATARINA: It can't be exactly so.
ROSITA: It struck the moment I came through the door.
CATARINA: Came through the door? When you were outside or in? On the first stroke or the tenth? How carelessly you express yourself. Didn't I tell you to call me so that I should hear the tenth stroke? I didn't hear it.
ROSITA: It's difficult, Dona Catarina. It's never really worked since my first year. Then I'd wait at the door for the fifth stroke before pressing down the handle. But I don't know how it came about, whether it was the clockwork that changed, or my patience. The fact is I couldn't bring it off any longer. And if I opened the door on the fourth stroke, there was the danger that a skin might form on the chocolate.
CATARINA: Disgusting!
ROSITA: To tell you the truth, it's been getting worse and worse every year. In fact more than once I've had palpitations when I reached the door.
CATARINA: I expect there are other reasons for that, Rosita. You were

104

seventeen when you came to me, and you've been with me for five years. It's the age for strong palpitations.

ROSITA: Not only palpitations, though. My teeth chatter too, and I'm afraid I shall drop the tray.

CATARINA: Your symptoms bore me. And I never heard anything like it from your predecessor, who was in my service for twelve years.

ROSITA: That's no wonder, Dona Catarina, since she had no teeth left.

CATARINA: Enough small talk. Remove the cup. The weather?

ROSITA: Dull.

CATARINA: The sea?

ROSITA: Rolling as ever.

CATARINA: Quiet! *(A pause)* Yes, it's rolling as ever. That's a comfort. Do you know how I feel when I hear that sound?

ROSITA: You've told me, Dona Catarina: nearer to God.

CATARINA: How unspeakably silly that sounds when you say it.

ROSITA: It sounds silly as — *(She stops short, startled.)*

CATARINA: As what?

ROSITA: No, nothing.

CATARINA: Sometimes there's something insolent about you — a rebellious strain.

ROSITA *(candidly)*: Oh, no; certainly not.

CATARINA: What's that stain on the coverlet? Everything is getting spoiled and filthy, because you girls pay no attention.

ROSITA: It's red wine, Dona Catarina; yesterday's.

CATARINA *(taken aback)*: Red wine? My own doing? *(Since Rosita keeps silent)* How much did I drink?

ROSITA: You left the dregs of two litres.

CATARINA *(sadly)*: Well, I left the dregs anyway. *(After a pause)* The strange thing is that I couldn't bear to hear it at first. I used to put my hands over my ears.

ROSITA: The rolling sea, you mean?

CATARINA: It seemed like the very epitome of my exile. Oh, my ears were full of gay laughter from the royal palace, tender words from the trellised walks in the park, verses —

ROSITA: Today's poem is: 'On the Banks of the Mondego he thinks of his Natercia.'

CATARINA: But twenty-seven years are enough to transmute the crackle of Hell's flames into the soothing murmur of divine forgiveness.

ROSITA *(uncertain)*: You're quoting?

CATARINA: To transmute hatred into love.

ROSITA: And the love into what, if I may make so free as to ask?

CATARINA: You may not make so free. *(She sobs.)*

ROSITA *(helpless)*: Dona Catarina!

CATARINA *(calmly)*: What poem?

ROSITA: The third in Volume II.

CATARINA: Don't pretend you can read. Pedro is having no end of trouble with you.

ROSITA: And so are you, Dona Catarina.

CATARINA: I must admit, my child, that it isn't one of the regular duties of a lady's maid to recite verses. Stand over there, next to the wardrobe.

ROSITA: And gaze out of the window on to the sea.

CATARINA: Don't say it, Rosita, do it!

ROSITA: Few days divide us: seven to speak plain.
　　Like seven waves they travel with the tide,
　　Mere flecks upon those waters deep and wide,
　　As endlessly I tell myself — in vain!

　　For I can set no limits to the pain
　　Of this brief span of absence; nor abide
　　The single glance, the single kiss denied,
　　And of their lack most grievously complain.

　　No measure now is valid, but thine own,
　　Natercia, for eternity and time,
　　The glance, the kiss, the grief that fills my rhyme.

　　Both clock and calendar I have outgrown,
　　The very sun and moon thine eyes eclipse:
　　Eternity begins upon thy lips.

CATARINA: Eternity — all right. But twenty-seven years?

ROSITA: It's difficult to recite something one doesn't understand.

CATARINA: It's because you don't understand it that you have the ability. You recite the poem excellently, my child.

ROSITA: In that case it must be the wardrobe, and the oblique view of the sea.

CATARINA: Why don't you understand it, by the way? How could

106

anyone fail to understand it?

ROSITA: I don't understand the feelings he's put into rhymes.

CATARINA *(disconcerted)*: Oh? *(After a pause)* There really is something rebellious about you. Ideas of that kind are not fitting for servants.

ROSITA: I beg your pardon, Dona Catarina.

CATARINA: Oh, fiddlesticks! Let's begin a revolutionary conversation. So the rhymes —

ROSITA: And Natercia. Why does he say Natercia, when your name is. Catarina?

CATARINA: In the course of the years I've begun to wonder whether my name isn't Natercia.

ROSITA: But at that time —

CATARINA: Yes, true enough, at that time my name was still Catarina. We must proceed methodically, my child. The rhymes and Natercia are two entirely different matters. We mustn't confuse them. The point of the rhymes is that they're contrary to nature.

ROSITA *(uncomprehending)*: Ah!

CATARINA: Because human virtue begins where God's creature rises above mere crude nature. What do feelings amount to, after all? Skin rubbing against skin; the milkmaids and the mill-hands do that too. It's only when feelings begin to rhyme, Rosita; that's something.

ROSITA: Ah!

CATARINA: Do you follow me? (ROSITA *is silent.*) I can read the questions in your obdurate eyes. How unseemly a pretty face becomes when it stares at an older one, how coarse! Imagine me holding my nose and lifting the hem of my dress as I go down the steps in the yard, where the pigs squelch and slobber over their troughs, and the mules drop their apples.

ROSITA: Yes, Dona Catarina, for our sort there is only nature.

CATARINA: And for me too, Rosita, for me too. Don't be offended.

ROSITA: To go back to the pigs: we leave them in the dirt and blame them for stinking.

CATARINA *(taking no notice)*: No, I can find no rhymes, no more than you can. I am nothing, I am something only through him, near him, beside him, with him — far from him —

ROSITA *(condoling)*: Dear Dona Catarina ...

CATARINA: Never mind. It all comes from having allowed you to talk about rhymes. It didn't occur to me how dangerous a topic it is.

ROSITA: And Natercia?

CATARINA: I fear that's another. Well, let's try all the same. Remove the tray and begin to do my hair. What do you think of my hair?

ROSITA: It's very lovely still.

CATARINA *(doubtful)*: Do you think so? I fancy it looks as though the moths have got into it.

ROSITA: I think that hair and hair-styles are something I know quite a lot about.

CATARINA: That's your kind of rhyme.

ROSITA *(laughing happily)*: Yes, Dona Catarina.

CATARINA: On the other hand, he called me Natercia because no one was to know whom he meant by the name.

ROSITA: I see. No one knew, then?

CATARINA: At first no one knew.

ROSITA: And if he'd kept the poems to himself?

CATARINA: Rosita! Would he have become Portugal's greatest poet in that case? Should we be sitting here, talking about him?

ROSITA: No, but you might have had children and grandchildren now. *(Hurriedly, as though trying to blot out this sentence)* I can just imagine it. It would be just like when the hen has laid an egg. Shall I sweep up your hair higher still?
*(*CATARINA *utters a scream.*)*
Did I hurt you, Dona Catarina?

CATARINA: I can see the cup in the looking-glass.

ROSITA *(hurriedly)*: Perhaps we should try a new hair-style —

CATARINA: It's the cup with the lily pattern.

ROSITA: If we swept up your hair on the sides —

CATARINA *(sharply)*: I am speaking of the cup.

ROSITA *(uncertain)*: Yes, of course.

CATARINA: Well?

ROSITA: Yes, it's the cup with the lily pattern.

CATARINA: But I had ordered the rose pattern. Didn't Pedro tell you?

ROSITA: It's possible, madam.

CATARINA: Possible?

ROSITA: Or rather impossible. The cup with the rose pattern was broken — by my predecessor.

CATARINA: Your predecessor? You've been with me for five years. What you're telling me is that for just that time I've been living under the delusion that I drink my morning chocolate out of the rose cup.

ROSITA: Is that such a serious matter?

CATARINA: Not serious, but full of implications.

ROSITA: If I may make so free as to ask another question: Did he always call you Natercia?

CATARINA: That's strange, isn't it?

ROSITA: Who would think of such a thing! Only a poet.

CATARINA: I'm speaking of the cup, and the five years. The thought is like a mist, but one knows that everything will be clearer when it's lifted. What did you say about him?

ROSITA: Did he always call you Natercia?

CATARINA: In the poems, that goes without saying.

ROSITA: And elsewhere too, at times?

CATARINA: And elsewhere too at times.

ROSITA: I like the idea that he called you Natercia even when you were alone together. Though there was nothing to conceal then, and though it didn't rhyme with anything.

CATARINA (irritated): Yes, that's true. Why did he do it, in that case?

ROSITA: Perhaps because it was contrary to nature.

CATARINA: I'm beginning to confuse the name with the pattern on the cup.

ROSITA: Perhaps he did it for no reason at all.

CATARINA: For no reason?

ROSITA: Just like that — as a kind of game.

CATARINA (bewildered): A kind of game?

ROSITA: Your hair is done. How do you like it?

CATARINA: Call Pedro.

ROSITA (opens the door): Pedro!

CATARINA: Did we never mention the pattern on the cup in all these years?

ROSITA: Oh yes, Dona Catarina, but you never actually asked about it.

CATARINA: In that case I allowed myself to be deceived.

ROSITA: I didn't know it was so important to you.

CATARINA: Nor did I know it. (Pedro knocks and enters.) Well?

PEDRO: Dona Catarina?

CATARINA (furious): Dona Catarina in her dressing-gown! Just the right moment to choose for your faultless bows, for affected, secretarial phrases. The devil take you if you don't speak to the point.

PEDRO (confused): But what about, Dona Catarina?

CATARINA: About the lilies, about the roses! Pedro, I am being deceived.

109

PEDRO: Deceived, madam?

ROSITA: We're speaking of the cup.

CATARINA: For ten years I've been living in a state of delusion, and no one tells me.

PEDRO: Dona Catarina, it happened about seven years ago. The tray slipped out of the maid's hands.

CATARINA (*sharply*): We are speaking of the tenth of June, 1580, that is, rather more than ten years ago.

ROSITA: You even know the date! So you must have known, too, that I brought you the lily pattern every morning.

CATARINA: That morning, so they said, Luiz Vaz de Camões died of the plague in Lisbon. Pedro, reflect on it, think of the delusions under which I live; and no one bothers to dispel them.

PEDRO: Dona Catarina, do you doubt for a moment —

CATARINA: Who said anything about doubts? Fetch some red wine, Rosita.

ROSITA: Before sundown?

CATARINA: This is an unusual day.

ROSITA: Very well, madam.

(Exit Rosita.)

CATARINA: Certainly, Pedro, that's it. The pattern on the cup has opened my eyes. How blindly we live on from day to day. Merely because we never ask anyone.

PEDRO: Dona Catarina, even if you ask me —

CATARINA: It's too late now, Pedro, you can't deceive me now. Sit down. We must discuss the details.

PEDRO: The pattern seemed insignificant to me.

CATARINA: As insignificant as the plague of which Camões died. The details of the journey, Pedro!

PEDRO: But the King commanded you never to leave Setúbal.

CATARINA: Ten years lost, and you want me to lose more time? I know that Camões is alive, and I am going to see him.

PEDRO: Who's alive? See whom?

CATARINA: I believed in his death as I believed in the rose pattern. We are leaving for Lisbon.

On the terrace of Catarina's house.

PEDRO: At first I thought that this journey didn't fit in with our plans. But after a little reflection —

110

ROSITA: A good thing that you reflect. Personally I've given it up. Everything seems to black out when I start thinking. How can you bear it?

PEDRO: Bear it? What has that got to do with thinking? A man has to make decisions, hasn't he?

ROSITA: All right, you can take on the decisions. As for me, I'll take on the black-outs for you.

PEDRO: Don't be silly. Has Dona Catarina enough red wine?

ROSITA: Two litres. If that isn't enough, she'll ring.

PEDRO: I shall make it clear to her that we need a second coach. This journey is a stroke of luck for us. Like this we can even take things that would have been a great hindrance otherwise, things like the china, the heavy silver —

ROSITA: Oh, Pedro —

PEDRO: What?

ROSITA: The prospect of committing a theft is like a great expectation. I never thought that one day I may really be looking back on it.

PEDRO: Theft, you say? It's more than that. It's the whole matter of our life together, Rosita, and don't you forget it.

ROSITA: I don't forget it; but my conscience —

PEDRO: It would give me a bad conscience to leave such a lot of money and property in the hands of a madwoman. What does she need, after all! Red wine, bread and a bit of rolling sea.

ROSITA: Is she really mad? Listen, Pedro, the window is open, but can you hear anything?

PEDRO: What do you expect me to hear?

ROSITA: The rolling sea. Be quiet!

(Pause)

PEDRO: I can't hear anything.

ROSITA: That's just what I mean. I don't hear anything either. But she can hear it.

PEDRO: That's what proves that she's mad. She can hear the rolling sea, and is going off to Lisbon to visit a dead man.

ROSITA: I've never troubled to think whether he's alive or dead. But why shouldn't he be alive? Did anyone see him die?

PEDRO: He may be alive, for all I care. In that case he'll be enchanted to see his lovely Natercia again as an old hag smelling of red wine. Whether he's alive or dead, he gives us the opportunity to go to Lisbon and take possession of the treasures in this house. I'm ready to raise my hat to him or to shed a tear over his grave. In either case he'll help us to attain prosperity, and to do it soon, Rosita.

ROSITA: Rosita —

PEDRO: What do you mean?

ROSITA: Couldn't you perhaps call me by a different name for a change?

PEDRO: What different name? Don't you like the one you have?

ROSITA: All I mean is a different name.

PEDRO: For instance?

ROSITA: For instance: Natercia.

PEDRO: Natercia! *(He bursts out laughing.)*

ROSITA: I only gave it as an instance. I know the name sounds silly.

PEDRO: Then why —

ROSITA: But I should have been glad all the same if you'd called me that.

PEDRO: Natercia.

ROSITA: That or a different name.

PEDRO: Antonia, Inez, Esther, Francisca, Margarida, Maria —

ROSITA: Now it doesn't count any more.

PEDRO: Enough of these stupidities. You're too sentimental.

ROSITA: I'm not sentimental. I was only joking.
(A ring.)

PEDRO: It's the old girl.

ROSITA: And now I'm going to indulge in the joke of telling her that we intend to rob her.

PEDRO: Are you mad?

ROSITA: I have my duties towards Dona Catarina. What she expects of me is not only the chocolate and the red wine, but some sweetmeat to go with it. The customs officer's love affairs are her Madeira cake, stories about the bishop her macaroons. She eats too much sweet stuff.

PEDRO: Rosita, do you mean to say you're going to —
(Another ring.)

ROSITA: Something savoury, Pedro, a few cheese straws —
(She runs up the stairs.)

PEDRO *(calls after her)*: Rosita!

ROSITA *(knocks on Dona Catarina's door and enters)*: A little more wine, Dona Catarina?

CATARINA: There's enough left for a conversation with you. Sit on my bed.

ROSITA: Do you hear the rolling sea, Dona Catarina?

CATARINA: Of course. Altogether it's a fact that I've heard it more clearly since my hearing began to get weak. But what was I going to say to you?

ROSITA: Something about the journey perhaps?

CATARINA *(thoughtful)*: Yes, of course, that was it.

ROSITA: Or shall I tell you something? I know of something.

CATARINA: Fancy that.

ROSITA: You see, Pedro and I have got together —

CATARINA: You mustn't think I haven't noticed that. I've always had a subtle flair for the first stirrings of love.

ROSITA: Got together to rob you of all your wealth. We intend to make use of the journey to Lisbon to take possession of all your property.

CATARINA *(laughing)*: That's a good one.

ROSITA: Not only good, but true.

CATARINA: I can see through you, rascals that you are.

ROSITA: How do you mean that, Dona Catarina?

CATARINA: Just another attempt to prevent the journey. Admit it, Rosita.

ROSITA: I admit everything.

CATARINA: First you say the coach is too small, then the horses go lame, then the wheel is broken, then we have no money, and now you're going to rob me. If I weren't fond of you, I should be angry with you for this. Why are you taking part in the conspiracy against me?

ROSITA: What conspiracy?

CATARINA: Do you think I haven't noticed it? No matter, though, not another word about it. And not another word from you to keep me from going to Lisbon. Go ahead and rob me, you miserable little thieves, go ahead and rob me! *(She laughs.)*

In the open. The coach approaches at walking speed and stops.

PEDRO: The Golden Key, Dona Catarina.

CATARINA: So this is where it was. But the house is painted black. Was it at that time too?

ROSITA: An inn with black distemper on the walls? It's unbelievable. No, Dona Catarina, it's a coffin. Let's move on.

CATARINA: The golden sign goes well with it.

ROSITA: Coffins too have golden metal-work on them, if I remember rightly.

CATARINA: And the window-frames are white — it's in good taste, whatever else it may be. No objections, please, my timid little dove!

113

It's part of our itinerary to spend the night here. Hey there, landlord! (*To* PEDRO) Is it the same man as before?

PEDRO: He certainly wasn't as bent as that. I suppose it's because of his noble guests, who drag a man's head down to the ground.

LANDLORD (*approaching*): At your service, Your Grace, it's due to the passage of time, if I may take the liberty of having overheard. You have stopped at the Golden Key, as the sign tells you. The Golden Key, so the legend has it —

PEDRO: Thank you; we are looking for lodgings suitable for a lady.

LANDLORD: Look no further, then. Even if my rooms were bad, they're the only ones between Setúbal and Lisbon.

PEDRO: So the rooms are bad?

CATARINA: I remember now.

LANDLORD: I used the conditional tense.

CATARINA: It's by the conditional tense that I recognize him.

PEDRO: This is a lady of high rank with her attendants. Two coaches.

LANDLORD: So I observe. She will drown in leopard skins. We have Indian, African and Chinese rooms.

CATARINA: I remember more and more clearly. Even these words were uttered ten years ago.

LANDLORD: But ten years ago I was in the habit of adding: the windows overlook a world empire. They no longer overlook a world empire. That is why I chose black paint for the walls.

PEDRO: A patriot.

LANDLORD: It puts off a good many potential guests. But I am conscious of what I owe to my country's decline.

CATARINA: No doubt at all. It's the same man. Have the horses unharnessed, Pedro. Support me, Rosita.

LANDLORD: Your Grace will be satisfied.

CATARINA: For that I need something different from a leopard skin. But you could make a good start by advising the fleas to practise a little reticence.

LANDLORD: I shall pass on your order. And what else can I do for Your Grace?

CATARINA: Red wine in my room.

LANDLORD: At your service. It is excellent. I drink it myself.

CATARINA: Then you will drink it with me. I have something to discuss with you. Where are my rooms?

LANDLORD: The whole of the first floor is at your disposal.

114

CATARINA: Pedro will call you.

LANDLORD: At your service.

CATARINA: It appears that you don't recognize me?

LANDLORD: I have the feeling that I know you well, though I am sure that we have not met very often.

PEDRO: A diplomatic reply.

LANDLORD: But the truth all the same.

PEDRO: We said, ten years ago.

LANDLORD *(thinking hard)*: Ten years ago? That was a short time before I put on the black distemper, about the time when Camões died.

CATARINA: Has Camões died?

LANDLORD: Of the plague, in Lisbon. On the 10th of June 1580. I used to know him personally, went to India with him, and know his sonnets by heart —

ROSITA: No measure now is valid, but thine own, Natercia, for eternity and time —

LANDLORD: What? Do the young people know his verses? I shall cease to be anxious for Portugal. A good reason for changing the colour of my house to pink or green.

PEDRO: Don't be in too great a hurry.

LANDLORD: As for Natercia: Soon after a lady came here — *(he falters)* — a lady —

PEDRO: Natercia?

LANDLORD: Yes, indeed: Natercia. *(Deferential)* As I said, madam: I am entirely at your disposal.

CATARINA: Come, Rosita.

(*Exeunt* CATARINA *and* ROSITA.)

LANDLORD: A great day for my house. But, to be honest, somewhat confusing.

PEDRO: How so?

LANDLORD: The coaches would be safest in the yard.

PEDRO: I shall see to them myself.

LANDLORD: Something foolish has been done.

PEDRO: Something foolish?

LANDLORD: Not important, but very foolish all the same. Perhaps she won't notice.

PEDRO: May I know what it is?

LANDLORD: Hm.

PEDRO: Whatever it is, you may be sure that she'll ask a great many questions.

LANDLORD: I shall have it put right beforehand. I must hurry.

PEDRO *(calls after him)*: That's a fine way to behave — *(grumpily to himself)* to arouse a man's curiosity and then run away. Sometimes one would think that there's nothing but madmen in the world. The only one here who knows what he's doing is myself. Gee up! *(The coach rumbles off into the yard.)*

Room in the inn.

CATARINA: If you can recall it, I occupied this very room.

LANDLORD: I beg your pardon, madam, but I don't remember the details. Yet I can truthfully say that your visit itself was unforgettable.

CATARINA: It is the details that would interest me.

LANDLORD: You turned back because the plague was sweeping Lisbon.

CATARINA: That's wrong for a start: I turned back because I was informed that Camões had died.

LANDLORD: For that reason also. You had two reasons for turning back.

CATARINA: There's no such thing; it was one reason or two excuses.

LANDLORD: That seems too peremptory to me. Our acquaintance with the poets teaches us to appreciate the finer shades — don't you think, Dona Catarina?

CATARINA: The finer shades derive from good society. Poets who startle no one are good for nothing but to provide topics for conversation.

LANDLORD: You are anticipating — by three centuries, Dona Catarina. Let us remain where we are.

CATARINA: But only for one night at the Golden Key. I am on my way to Lisbon, to visit Luís Vaz de Camões.

LANDLORD: Luís Vaz de Camões.

CATARINA: That's a repetition; I expect an answer.

LANDLORD: If I may permit myself a correction: you are on your way to Lisbon to visit a grave.

CATARINA: So you won't admit it?

LANDLORD: What should I admit?

CATARINA: That, on the other hand, is a question, and still no answer.

LANDLORD: If I only knew what you have in mind?

CATARINA: Presumably you know it quite well. Is your collar too tight?

LANDLORD: A change in the weather. I respond to it in advance. Since I went to the tropics I've been sensitive to the weather. And my rheumatism —

116

CATARINA: You put too little trust in the power of red wine. Where is the grave which I intend to visit?

LANDLORD: Oh, I didn't mean it as exactly as that.

CATARINA: Exactness is something one learns from the poets. Didn't you tell me at that time that you had spent months under the same roof with him? You have confused him with one of his commentators. Well, where is the grave?

LANDLORD: I thought you knew that there isn't an actual grave.

CATARINA: What is it then?

LANDLORD: Those who died of the plague were buried in a communal grave.

CATARINA: How illuminating!

LANDLORD: And even there one has to depend on guesswork. There were so many dead and no one knew him.

CATARINA: Don't you think yourself that all this, to put it mildly, is a little vague?

LANDLORD: As definite as circumstances permitted. When I was in Lisbon two years later, I questioned his servant.

CATARINA: His servant is still alive?

LANDLORD: He was alive then in any case.

CATARINA: And?

LANDLORD: I don't know why I'm telling you this.

CATARINA: The change in the weather, your rheumatism. It will rain tomorrow, isn't that so?

LANDLORD: All I am telling you I have from him, and he knew no more than what I am telling you.

CATARINA: It's all very suspicious. Every word conceals something. What's the servant's name, and where does he live?

LANDLORD: A Javanese servant, Ojao by name. At that time he lived in the Travessa da Boa Hora.

CATARINA: I expect he has died in the meantime. All the evidence is most uncertain.

LANDLORD: It's conceivable too that a man should move house.

CATARINA: People who have nothing to conceal don't move house.

LANDLORD: I no longer dare to draw your attention to the finer shades.

CATARINA: All you know derives from this servant. But already two years before you questioned him you told me that Camões was dead. How did you know it then?

LANDLORD: Ojao confirmed what I already knew.

CATARINA: And how did you come to know it?

LANDLORD: I was told by the driver of the mail-coach, who went to Lisbon each week —

CATARINA: And what's his name?

LANDLORD: He was called Manuel Azevevo.

CATARINA: His address?

LANDLORD: He is dead; he fell off his coach box when drunk and —

CATARINA: Dead! That means that all the witnesses are inaccessible. Oh, what a fool I was ever to have believed you! Ten years lost!

LANDLORD: Dona Catarina, there is no reason to doubt the death of the honoured —

CATARINA: Yes, there is every reason. Nor do I believe that you only gave me unreliable information. You did it on purpose.

LANDLORD: I am deeply —

CATARINA: And rightly so. But your dismay is not good enough.

LANDLORD: Yet it is more than is compatible with my self-respect.

CATARINA: Where should we be if we considered the self-respect of toads?

LANDLORD: Dona Catarina, you are making our conversation a good deal easier for me. Until now I felt obliged to conceal something from you.

CATARINA: Indeed!

LANDLORD: I gave strict instructions to my staff that not a word was to be said about it, and, above all, that the name —

CATARINA: So you are confessing it at last!

LANDLORD: Yes, I am; I confess that I have called my donkey — a jenny — Natercia.

CATARINA: That you've called your donkey —

LANDLORD: Precisely, Dona Catarina! My donkey's name is Natercia. An uncommon name, but one made familiar by the great Camões. Don't you agree that it most aptly characterizes a stubborn attitude of mind?

CATARINA: Not really. You must have had a special reason for choosing it.

LANDLORD: If so, I wasn't aware of it till you spoke of toads.

CATARINA: Well, let me tell you the reason, then: because you were thinking of my stupidity in giving credence to you.

LANDLORD: I see that there are more possibilities than I reckoned with.

CATARINA: Do you deny it?

LANDLORD: There's something very plausible about your opinion.

CATARINA *(without paying attention to the mockery in his voice)*: What prevents you from being truthful is that you're joining in the conspiracy. You're all trying to conceal the fact that he's alive. Why not admit it?

LANDLORD: Every second Thursday in the month the conspirators meet in the Golden Key. Camões himself presides. We discuss the statutes and issue new directives. At the same time we eat and drink. You will understand that I am reluctant to forgo the profit which accrues to me from these items.

CATARINA: At first you tried what you could do by deferential readiness to serve, but I saw through you. Then I provoked you to insults, and I knew how to extract the truth even from these. Now you resort to mockery, with no more success than before. There remains one other course: see what you can do by accepting the truth for once.

LANDLORD *(with a sigh)*: Your truth, Dona Catarina. But in one regard I shall submit to you: I shall call my next donkey Felipe. For that happens to be my name. Really, I'm going round in a circle and pulling a whim-chain. But there's no question of either water or corn. It's a question of stones, Dona Catarina, and you think that they can be made to yield oil.

CATARINA *(almost imploring)*: Why don't you stop hedging!

LANDLORD *(sighing again)*: Very well, then. What is our reason for withholding the fact that Camões is alive?

CATARINA: Oh, but part of the conspiracy consists in concealing the reason for concealment.

LANDLORD *(somewhat exhausted)*: I see.

CATARINA: Now you're beginning to understand.

LANDLORD: And for what reason does Camões himself withhold it from you?

CATARINA: If you can only grasp it, this very circumstance proves the existence of a conspiracy.

LANDLORD: No, I cannot grasp it.

CATARINA: You insist on controverting all the arguments. Do stop hedging at last, make a clean breast.

LANDLORD *(gasping)*: I have, madam, I have. You may not believe me, but it was a physical strain. It seems that to stop hedging is to leap over an abyss.

CATARINA: And now?

119

LANDLORD: Now I'm in the open; but it's a most arid landscape.

CATARINA: Well, just pay attention for a moment, Don Felipe.

LANDLORD *(groaning)*: It's the change in the weather, you see.

CATARINA: There is no proof at all that Camões is dead.

LANDLORD: I admit that the information —

CATARINA: All the information is second- or third-hand. That means it's worthless. No one saw him die.

LANDLORD: True enough.

CATARINA: From that I conclude that he's alive.

LANDLORD: Certainly it is difficult to prove the contrary.

CATARINA: Didn't I tell you so!

LANDLORD: To be sure, he could be ill, perhaps incapable of communicating with you —

CATARINA: Ill, did you say? Of course. That's the explanation.

LANDLORD: Not so fast, Dona Catarina. I'm too short of breath for conclusions of that kind. I never said a word about his being ill.

CATARINA: So you think I'm deaf as well as —

LANDLORD: Dona Catarina, I'm prepared to admit anything you like. And yet my advice is: Turn back tomorrow.

CATARINA: What? You presume to suggest I should not go to Lisbon?

LANDLORD: Today it's like ten years ago, Dona Catarina. The plague is in Lisbon again, it forestalled you.

CATARINA: Well, this time the scare won't prevent me. *(Laughing)* The plague, a dangerous illness, what! A marvellous illness to prevent someone from going on a journey! An illness of which Camões has already died! The plague, Don Felipe, is an invention. There's no such thing as the plague, either in Lisbon or anywhere else. There never was such a thing! You may as well give up trying, for you won't deceive me again. *(Laughing more and more loudly)* The plague, the plague, who ever heard —
(Fade out.)

In the ante-room.

ROSITA: The plague, Pedro, the plague!

PEDRO: I heard it, Rosita. Now get away from the keyhole.

ROSITA: We must talk her out of it, Pedro.

PEDRO: She doesn't suspect the least thing. There's no danger.

ROSITA: No danger, you say?

PEDRO: Go in and tell her that I've hidden her jewels under the coach-box. Her confidence in me will be all the greater.

ROSITA: But what about the hundreds, the thousands of people who've died of the plague?

PEDRO: Oh, but think of how many have *not* died of the plague.

ROSITA: Be sensible, Pedro.

PEDRO: Be sensible, Rosita.

ROSITA: We must turn back.

PEDRO: Tell Dona Catarina, then.

ROSITA: No, even if she won't.

PEDRO: We shall go to Lisbon, even if she refuses to go. The matter is settled.

ROSITA: But if the circumstances demand —

PEDRO: I'm not a crab.

ROSITA: There's such a thing as a wrong decision.

PEDRO: Enough of that. The thought of spending a night sitting up in the coach is bad enough —

ROSITA: What a ridiculous precaution!

PEDRO: All the same; those gold coins weigh on me. That's a pleasing thought, displeasing though it may be. The plague, on the other hand —

ROSITA: I'm quite sure that in Lisbon you'll look very carefully at your finger-tips.

PEDRO: The plague is an invention of landlords, as Dona Catarina very rightly observed. Altogether her arguments are a great deal better than yours.

ROSITA: Aren't you worried on my account?

PEDRO: One's first worry is always for oneself. That shows you how sure I am.

ROSITA: A pity.

PEDRO: It was a pity that I didn't call you Natercia. Oh, my dear little jenny — when the night will be hard enough for me, why do you try to spoil the day as well? Think of our future, of our wealth —

ROSITA: I think of it continually, and can never help thinking of Dona Catarina's poverty at the same time.

PEDRO: Quite correct. One follows from the other. But don't forget that she'll have her red wine still, and an inexhaustible store of dreams.

ROSITA: I don't think her dreams are pleasant ones. You know how often she screams, how often she wakes me up —

PEDRO: And how often you have to call me. The devil take her if she doesn't leave us in peace tonight.

Dona Catarina's bedroom at the Golden Key

CATARINA: Rosita, Rosita! Extraordinary how these young things can sleep! No wonder her intelligence is deficient. Rosita!

ROSITA: Madam?

CATARINA: You forgot to open the window.

ROSITA: It is open, Dona Catarina.

CATARINA: Then why don't I hear the rolling sea?

ROSITA: Because we are not at Setúbal.

CATARINA: That's not a good reason, but still —

ROSITA: But what?

CATARINA: My dressing-gown, and help me out of bed.

ROSITA: It must be about three o'clock.

CATARINA: A good time of day.

ROSITA: For what?

CATARINA: For thieves. Didn't you know that? We shall creep through the house on stockinged feet. Come one.
(*The door opens.*)

ROSITA: Where to, Dona Catarina? And in the middle of the night?

CATARINA: Are you afraid?

ROSITA: Perhaps there's a dog in the house.

CATARINA: The door to the yard should be unlocked, don't you think?

ROSITA: Do you want to go out into the yard, Dona Catarina?

CATARINA: Just a breath of fresh air.
(*They open the door to the yard.*)
Stars, a moon. Our two coaches are well illuminated. Really they look quite imposing, quite inviting — out there in the open

ROSITA: Do you think, then — you spoke of thieves a little while ago — Pedro, too, thought it was incautious to —

CATARINA: Did he think so? What would we do without Pedro? In that case I dare say it's Pedro sitting there in the coach?

ROSITA: It is.

CATARINA: Well fancy that. I thought it was a thief.

ROSITA: No, it's Pedro.

CATARINA: Shall we try to steal something? I'm sure he won't notice. He's snoring.

ROSITA: Steal something?

CATARINA: A string of pearls, a brocade gown, a bag of ducats; why, we could extract a whole fortune from under the seat, and he wouldn't notice it.

ROSITA: A pity there's no fortune under the seat.

CATARINA: Yes, you're right. It isn't worth while, especially since I have more important business to attend to here.

ROSITA: What important business could there be in this yard at three o'clock in the morning?

CATARINA: A visit, Rosita.

ROSITA: You're perfectly right: a very good hour.

CATARINA: I started up from my sleep because I neglected all the proprieties. Isn't it proper to call on one's namesake?

ROSITA (giggling): I think you're overdoing the formalities, Dona Catarina.

CATARINA: Don't laugh, you silly thing. I don't think it at all impossible that Natercia feels offended.

ROSITA: Natercia?

CATARINA: Where's the stable door?

ROSITA: Couldn't it have been you who had reason to feel offended?

CATARINA: Am I not Natercia?

ROSITA: What a lot of questions. This could be it.

(They open the stable door, which creaks slightly.)

CATARINA: What can you see?

ROSITA: Hens, I think. Wait till my eyes have got used to it.

CATARINA: What else?

ROSITA: Sacks of barley.

CATARINA: That sounds right. (Listening) Do you hear something?

ROSITA: Something is stirring in the stalls. Could it be our horses?

CATARINA: Or Don Felipe's jenny. (She calls out softly.) Natercia!

ROSITA (likewise): Natercia!

CATARINA: Natercia!

ROSITA: There's a clattering noise in the stall.

CATARINA: Natercia!

(The donkey utters a piercing cry.)

CATARINA: That's enough, Rosita. Let's go.

ROSITA: Goodness, what a fright that animal gave me.

(She closes the stable door.)

CATARINA: It was a plain answer.

ROSITA: You're looking pale, Dona Catarina.

123

CATARINA: It's the moon, Rosita.

ROSITA: You're shivering.

CATARINA: Sometimes the nights are cool.

ROSITA: Yes.

CATARINA: I hope it hasn't woken our friend Pedro.

ROSITA: I don't suppose that would matter much.

CATARINA: What did you think of when the donkey cried?

ROSITA: Nothing. It made me jump.

CATARINA: Nor did I think of anything. It startled me too.

ROSITA: We should go to bed.

CATARINA: But when I heard that cry I suddenly knew that we're all going to die.

ROSITA *(constrained)*: There's nothing new about that.

CATARINA: No, but I've only just discovered it.

ROSITA: Of course we're all going to die.

CATARINA: Yes, even the one over there, in the coach.

(A pause. Then the coach starts, the horses trot, the whip cracks. The sounds fade.)

A narrow room.

OJAO: It was about six o'clock in the morning, and I went to the harbour to buy cod.

CATARINA: You again; but I want to know what *he* did. On the 10th of June 1580; you know which day I mean.

OJAO: The cod is not without importance either. Do you never take lunch, madam?

CATARINA: We are now at six o'clock in the morning.

OJAO: I have already said so. And that morning it was the bells that said so.

CATARINA: Six o'clock is not the only time the bells peal.

OJAO: True enough. A noisy religion, this one to which I've been converted! Bells and cannonades. I come from Java, Dona Catarina.

CATARINA: Firstly, you're a bad Christian. Secondly, Java is too far a digression. What did Don Luis say when you went out?

OJAO: He said nothing.

CATARINA: Was he still asleep?

OJAO: He was not asleep, nor was he awake.

CATARINA: Rosita, here you see someone capable of answering

questions even more badly than you do.

ROSITA: In that case Don Luis shared your fate in many ways, Dona Catarina.

CATARINA: Where did you get that from, Rosita? These young people! They've hardly reached the capital, and here they are rattling it off like the natives. Well, what didn't Don Luis say, then?

OJAO: He groaned. I made him some tea out of magnolia leaves.

ROSITA: Magnolia?

OJAO: Leaves. A recipe from Java.

ROSITA: That most certainly could do him no good. Where is this place, Java?

OJAO: It's a country — oh, palm trees, the odour of cinnamon.

CATARINA: Stop! Stop! We are talking of Don Luis.

OJAO: I was with him for ten years. I lay beside him on the decks of ships, on the bare boards, when the sails were tattered. At receptions I kept my distance, in the prisons I was close to him. I washed his clothes, cleaned his shoes, I —

CATARINA: And what did you do on that day?

OJAO: When he had drunk a little — he found it difficult to swallow — I put down the jug near the straw.

CATARINA: What straw?

OJAO: Near the straw on which he lay.

ROSITA: A Javanese custom?

OJAO: Not exclusively Javanese. Practised wherever there is poverty and straw.

CATARINA: Poverty?

OJAO: The poverty had come of itself. As for the straw, I had stolen it from the royal stables, and picked the magnolias on the river-banks — and I would obtain our fish by begging around the harbour.

CATARINA: What did I eat on the 10th of June 1580?

ROSITA: I wasn't in your service then.

CATARINA: How fortunate! Then I can say that I was fasting.

OJAO: I had to go there at six in the morning, for that was the most favourable hour. At that time I was likely to meet a fisherman who valued the poems of Don Luis. An uncommonly stingy fellow, unfortunately.

CATARINA: And Don Luis remained all alone?

OJAO: The people in the house passed by from time to time, on their way to the cellar. We were living in a recess under the cellar stairs. When I went out —

CATARINA: At six. Don Luis on the straw —

OJAO: He was quite brown already.

CATARINA: Brown?

OJAO: Dark brown. The plague.

CATARINA: And you?

OJAO: I had it in Java.

ROSITA: So there are people who don't die of it?

OJAO: Not many, but it does happen. Perhaps I was spared so as to be able to answer your questions.

CATARINA: One must bear in mind that it does happen.

OJAO: I was in luck that day. I got two cod heads. Perhaps, I thought to myself, Don Luis would eat some after all.

CATARINA: And did he?

OJAO: He died before I had cooked them.

CATARINA: Steady there, not so fast! You came back —

OJAO: He was hardly breathing.

CATARINA: Had he drunk anything?

OJAO: I think he was too weak. I moistened his lips.

CATARINA: And then you cooked the fish?

OJAO: I could see that it wasn't the right moment to cook fish. I stayed with Don Luis.

CATARINA: And — when — ?

OJAO: About an hour later.

CATARINA: That was at —

OJAO: It was about nine when I got back from the harbour. It must have happened just before ten. Soon after closing his eyes I heard the bells. And soon after that I heard the plague rattle. The cart was passing near by. I ran out and called the corpse-bearers. They put him on the cart.

CATARINA: With the others.

OJAO: With the others.

CATARINA: Where did the cart go?

OJAO: At that moment I felt sick. I vomited and then dragged myself to the cellar. There I slept till the evening.

CATARINA: Do you mean to say you didn't see where Don Luis was buried?

OJAO: No, but he died in my arms.

CATARINA: So I've been told already. The strange thing, however, is that he did not die at all.

OJAO: What?

CATARINA: You heard what I said. Don Luis is alive. How could he be, when he died in your arms? Or is it possible that you were mistaken?

OJAO *(confused)*: Could I have been mistaken? But where is Don Luis? Why doesn't he come?

CATARINA: Could you have been mistaken?

OJAO: If he's alive, I may have made a mistake. Let him come.

CATARINA: He will come when we know the truth.

OJAO: I wasn't so difficult. I went to Portugal with him. A strange country, to put it mildly, and I don't believe that it contains more truth than Java. Why does he hide from me?

CATARINA: Yes, why does he?

OJAO *(pensive)*: If he's still alive, he could be either with you

CATARINA: Or else?

OJAO: Or else at his mother's.

CATARINA: At his mother's?

OJAO: Yet it would be extraordinary if she'd been able to conceal it from me. Very little that happens in this district is concealed from me for long.

CATARINA: So she lives in the same district? I didn't know she was still alive.

OJAO: She is eighty, perhaps even ninety.

CATARINA: But since he died in your arms, how can you assume that he's at his mother's?

OJAO: It was you who said he's alive.

CATARINA: So you must have made a mistake. Admit it.

OJAO: One is reluctant to retract an assertion which one has repeated for ten years. Nevertheless, for Don Luis —

CATARINA: It is honourable to admit an error.

OJAO: But is it honourable, too, to admit a lie?

CATARINA: A lie?

OJAO: Don Luis will forgive me. For if you take it all too literally, he didn't die in my arms. He was still alive when I went to the harbour, that much is certain.

CATARINA: And when you returned?

OJAO: When I returned? I must add that I was a little late.

CATARINA: A little? When did you return?

OJAO: I met a girl, and we ate fish together. It must have been the early afternoon.

CATARINA: Not before the evening, you mean!

OJAO: I admit that it was growing dark.

CATARINA: And when you got back he was dead?

OJAO: He was neither alive nor dead. He was gone.

CATARINA: Gone? Gone out?

OJAO: They said he had died towards noon, and the plague cart had removed him. But it's possible too —

CATARINA: What's possible?

OJAO: You can imagine that people don't like to think that there's a man sick of the plague in their house. So it's possible, too —

CATARINA: That they had him removed before —

OJAO: That is the possibility which your words suggest to me.

ROSITA: Only a few more questions, and you will have brought him back to life, Dona Catarina.

CATARINA: Now to his mother's. Lead us there, Ojao.

(Pause)

Another room.

MOTHER: Dona Catarina de Ataide. Yes, I know your name. You brought my son no luck.

CATARINA: Does he say so? I should have thought —

MOTHER: I say so. But the young people are so high-spirited, they don't know what to do with themselves. A capricious person. Red-haired, are you not?

CATARINA: Fair.

OJAO: Where does this door lead, Dona Antonia?

MOTHER: Where should it lead, imbecile? Into the underworld, otherwise known as the cellar.

OJAO: Why did you say underworld?

CATARINA: Yes, that's suspicious.

OJAO: It's behind that door we should look, isn't it, Dona Antonia?

MOTHER: Of course it is. Where else would it be?

OJAO: We've got him.

ROSITA: The cellar is what Dona Antonia means.

MOTHER: What are you chattering about? You must raise your voices.

CATARINA: Does Don Luis come to see you every day, Dona Antonia?

128

MOTHER: Without fail.

CATARINA: Does he live with you?

MOTHER: It seems as though he lived with me and as though he were still alive. We discuss everything. He told me that he had to keep away from Court because of you, Dona Catarina. Why were you at Court?

ROSITA: Dona Catarina was lady-in-waiting to Her Majesty the Queen.

MOTHER *(tenderly)*: He was a ne'er-do-well, that Luis. Later he wrote verses.

ROSITA: Even at that time he did. Natercia —

CATARINA: Hold your tongue. *(To the mother)* I should like to speak to Don Luis too.

MOTHER: Then he fought a duel, also because of you. You're responsible for everything. India, China, Madagascar, a musket shot in his left eye, prison, exile — it's all your fault. If only I could see better — I should really like to take a good look at this red-haired person who was the ruin of him. Step closer, my daughter.

CATARINA *(mumbling)*: Don't imagine I haven't suffered. Twenty-seven years of Setúbal —

MOTHER: Oh yes, I can imagine it now. The pretty masks women wear when they're young!

CATARINA: So you see me with his eyes?

MOTHER: Yes, I see you with his eyes.

CATARINA: It's true, isn't it? He still lives.

MOTHER: He will live for ever, my daughter.

OJAO: Come, Dona Catarina. He's behind this door.

MOTHER: Where are you going? It's pitch-black down there. Are you going to count my cabbages?

(OJAO *and* DONA CATARINA *go down to the cellar.*)

MOTHER: Now I want you to talk. You seem to be the most sensible of the three.

ROSITA: I'm Dona Catarina's lady's maid.

MOTHER: What do those two want in my cellar?

ROSITA: They're looking for Don Luis.

MOTHER *(happy)*: Well, as it happens, he really is in the cellar.

ROSITA: So Dona Catarina is right after all. I should never have thought so.

MOTHER: But they won't find him.

ROSITA: He must be clever at hiding.

MOTHER: He's not hiding at all. But if they didn't see him up here, they won't see him down there either.

ROSITA: Was he up here, then, all the time?

MOTHER: Certainly. Didn't he talk to you all?

ROSITA: I didn't hear anything.

MOTHER: He was sitting next to me, on this stool.

ROSITA: Oh?

MOTHER: Naturally he wasn't sitting on the stool either, but on the bench.

ROSITA: And at the same time he was in the cellar?

MOTHER: At last you've seen what I mean.

ROSITA: Not quite. I should like to know whether my poor mistress

MOTHER: She will see him, never worry.

(Ojao and Dona Catarina return.)

MOTHER *(cheerfully)*: Well?

CATARINA: It's uncommonly dark down there.

MOTHER: Didn't I tell you?

OJAO: But light enough to see —

ROSITA: See what?

MOTHER: My son, perhaps? Is he down there?

OJAO: Nothing. Dona Catarina, what was the use of admitting my lie?

CATARINA: It was so dark that I learned to understand darkness.

MOTHER: An excellent thing!

CATARINA: Come on, Rosita. The old woman is mocking us, and I know why.

MOTHER: Since I'm not mocking anyone, you can hardly know why.

CATARINA: The truth is I'm too old, too ugly for him. The cellar has a door that leads outside. He is running away from me. He is hiding from me. Now everything is clear to me, Rosita. He himself is at the heart of the conspiracy. He himself made sure that I should receive the news that he is dead; it was he himself.

ROSITA: He himself?

CATARINA: Let's go Rosita.

In the Palace.

LORD CHAMBERLAIN: Dona Catarina de Ataide.

CATARINA: Yes, I'm coming.

LORD CHAMBERLAIN: His Majesty regrets that he cannot receive you.

CATARINA: The matter is of great importance.

LORD CHAMBERLAIN: If it were not, you would not have requested an audience.

130

CATARINA: That is so.

LORD CHAMBERLAIN: His Majesty regrets —

CATARINA: So you said. Tomorrow perhaps?

LORD CHAMBERLAIN: You might try tomorrow.

(A pause.)

The scene changes.

CATARINA: Dona Catarina de Ataide requests an audience.

LORD CHAMBERLAIN: His Majesty regrets —

CATARINA: I made the same request yesterday. His Majesty appears not to remember that my family is among the most prominent in the country.

LORD CHAMBERLAIN: His Majesty does remember, but nevertheless regrets —

CATARINA: So you said.

LORD CHAMBERLAIN: Perhaps tomorrow.

CATARINA: The matter in question, you see, is my banishment.

LORD CHAMBERLAIN: Very well.

CATARINA: Nearly thirty years ago now, I was forbidden to return to Lisbon.

LORD CHAMBERLAIN: But now you have returned.

CATARINA: To beg the King —

LORD CHAMBERLAIN: You were right to return, and could have done so twenty years sooner.

CATARINA: No one told me anything about that.

LORD CHAMBERLAIN: Because your banishment was forgotten about long ago.

CATARINA: Unfortunately I did not forget it. I took the King's word to be a royal word.

LORD CHAMBERLAIN: Did I say anything to the contrary?

CATARINA: Yes, you did.

LORD CHAMBERLAIN: A misunderstanding, Dona Catarina. Well, however that may be, you can rely on me. The King will revoke your banishment.

CATARINA: You have overlooked that I myself have already revoked it.

LORD CHAMBERLAIN: But it was not your intention to —

CATARINA: The request I now have to make is a different one.

LORD CHAMBERLAIN: Would you not perhaps confide — ? My position naturally places me close to the King.

131

CATARINA: To you? *(Hesitant)* The fact is —

LORD CHAMBERLAIN *(encouragingly)*: Do proceed.

CATARINA: When I was banished thirty years ago, I was still young.

LORD CHAMBERLAIN: If it is any consolation to you, Dona Catarina, none of us has grown any younger during these thirty years.

CATARINA: It is no consolation to me. For I was not only young I was beautiful.

LORD CHAMBERLAIN: Dona Catarina, I can see it still.

CATARINA: But Don Luis Vaz de Camões does not see it.

LORD CHAMBERLAIN: Camões? The poet?

CATARINA: He avoids meeting me.

LORD CHAMBERLAIN: I was under the impression that he is dead.

CATARINA: Mere rumours! I know the truth.

LORD CHAMBERLAIN: Well, maybe. And I happen to have little interest in poetry. Personally I collect butterflies.

CATARINA: And now I wanted to beg the King, since he banished me and took away thirty years of my life — it was all at his command, you see.

LORD CHAMBERLAIN: I do see.

CATARINA: I wanted to beg the King to give me back my beauty.

LORD CHAMBERLAIN: To give you back your beauty?

CATARINA: Yes.

LORD CHAMBERLAIN *(reflective)*: Beauty. That, certainly, is something which only the King himself can decide.

CATARINA: Yes, I thought so too. That's why I presumed that an audience —

LORD CHAMBERLAIN: Very well, I shall see.

CATARINA: Perhaps tomorrow?

LORD CHAMBERLAIN: Yes. You might try tomorrow.

(A pause.)

The scene changes.

CATARINA: Dona Catarina de Ataide begged His Majesty for an audience — but I assume that today also His Majesty regrets —

LORD CHAMBERLAIN: Oh no, Dona Catarina.

CATARINA: You mean I can see the King?

LORD CHAMBERLAIN: I beg you to follow me, Dona Catarina. I am taking you to the throne-room.

(They go through doors, along passages and stairs.)

132

CATARINA: It's all been rebuilt. But for you, I shouldn't have found my way any more. Or perhaps it's simply too long ago.

LORD CHAMBERLAIN: Most probably it's simply too long ago.

(They stop.)

LORD CHAMBERLAIN: The throne-room, Dona Catarina.

(He opens a door.)

CATARINA: But —

LORD CHAMBERLAIN: What were you going to say, Dona Catarina?

CATARINA: That is no throne — that's a coffin!

LORD CHAMBERLAIN: His Majesty the King died early this morning of the plague.

(Outside bells begin to ring. They come to a crescendo.)

The scene changes to the open air.

ROSITA: Dona Catarina, did you speak to the King?

CATARINA: He was very gracious, Rosita. Where's Pedro, where's the coach?

ROSITA: I'm glad you spoke to the King. Because, you see —

CATARINA: What?

ROSITA: I mean, in that case perhaps it won't be quite so bad.

CATARINA: What won't be?

ROSITA: You see, Dona Catarina, there isn't a coach any more, and no Pedro.

CATARINA: But you're still here.

ROSITA: Yes, I'm still here.

CATARINA: We shall have to go on foot.

ROSITA: Yes.

CATARINA: I am very glad that you are still here. Don't worry about it. If we want to return to Setúbal, it's really a good thing to be rid of all that troublesome luggage.

ROSITA: If you look at it that way, Dona Catarina —

CATARINA: That's the way I look at it.

(A pause.)

In the open air — on the ferry.

CATARINA: Farewell, Lisbon, hill above the Tejo —

ROSITA: A good day for our crossing, plenty of wind in the sails.

CATARINA: And the dolphins are playing. One would so much like to see a connection between the weather and the leave-taking. Farewell, Lisbon.

ROSITA: The sky so blue!

CATARINA: The sky blue or grey — every colour doubles the pain. I know it, Rosita: the weather itself is a kind of leave-taking. Why don't you wave?

ROSITA: Whom should I wave to?

CATARINA: To the sky, the dolphins, the children on the shore. But you don't wave because you're hiding your hands.

ROSITA: Why should I be hiding my hands?

CATARINA: The King's face was black as he lay on his catafalque. I don't think they will lay him out in the Cathedral. But I'm not thinking of the King, I'm thinking of you. I noticed that you're looking at your finger-tips in secret.

ROSITA: You must have made a mistake, Dona Catarina. I am not looking at my fingers — I'm not afraid.

CATARINA: And neither should you be. I gathered that this time far fewer people died than ten years ago.

ROSITA: Yes, it isn't so bad this time.

CATARINA: Show me your hands.

ROSITA: There you are: as white as could be!

CATARINA: True enough, as white as could be. It's hardly credible.

ROSITA: Why, didn't you expect them to be?

CATARINA: Of course I did.

ROSITA (laughing): And your hands, Dona Catarina?

CATARINA: Quiet, girl — so that the crew won't throw me overboard at this stage — so near the shore.

ROSITA: Why — ?

CATARINA: Isn't it enough that I don't show them to you, Rosita?

ROSITA: I understand.

CATARINA: But believe me if I tell you that I didn't notice it till we were on the ferry. Or I should never have asked you to come with me.

ROSITA: It doesn't matter, Dona Catarina.

CATARINA: Turn back; take the same boat back.

ROSITA: Where to?

CATARINA: To Pedro. It would be a comfort to me to know that you are provided for.

ROSITA: It would be no comfort to me. You see, Dona Catarina, I ceased to be afraid of the plague when I found out that it exists.

CATARINA: You'll have to repeat that at some other time. I believe it's the sentence in which the world begins for me. Anyway, it's a royal

134

plague; I touched the purple on the coffin.

ROSITA: In that case I can assume that, for reasons of rank alone, the plague will pass me by.

CATARINA: Nevertheless I order you always to keep at a distance of three paces. One can't be sure that the aristocratic distinctions are universally observed.

(The ship's bell rings. Fade out.)

At the Golden Key.

LANDLORD: Wife, wife!

WIFE: No need to shout so loud. I'm no more asleep than you are.

LANDLORD: And in your case it isn't the weather. What is it, then?

WIFE: It's the moon, because it shines so brightly into the room. Or else the dogs in the distance. And the animals too are stirring in the stable, rattling their chains. And why aren't you asleep?

LANDLORD: I was just thinking how the Golden Key is falling to pieces. It's hardly worth carrying on.

WIFE: Soon the white distemper will show through again through the black. That will be an advantage in some ways.

LANDLORD: And then I was thinking what I should say when I'm questioned at the Last Judgment. There's so little solid evidence one can present.

WIFE: Well, there's time enough to think about that. Besides, they're unlikely to ask about the Golden Key of all things. An inn counts about as much and as little as a feeding trough or the royal sceptre.

LANDLORD: I know that. And I'm not talking about ultimate values.

WIFE: What are you talking about, then?

LANDLORD: My rheumatism. Wife, it isn't the rain that I feel in my bones, it's the angels and their swords.

WIFE: Don't trouble your head about it, Felipe — it all comes of your mixing with poets.

LANDLORD: Can't you hear it?

WIFE: The last trumpet, I suppose.

LANDLORD: No, someone clapping his hands. Quiet!

WIFE: I hear something too.

LANDLORD: Let's get up and light up the house. I knew it would come tonight.

WIFE: It's your addiction to dramatic effects, Felipe. What's coming tonight?

135

LANDLORD: My rheumatism. And later, perhaps, some guests.

WIFE: What about opening the window?

LANDLORD: A good idea. *(He opens the window and calls out.)* Hallo?

ROSITA *(outside)*: Don Felipe! Landlord!

LANDLORD: Who is it? *(Softly, to his wife)* Two women.

ROSITA: Dona Catarina and her maid.

LANDLORD: Ah! One moment, please. I'm coming down. Where's your coach?

ROSITA: We've come on foot.

WIFE: Ladies, and travelling on foot. Did you hear that?

ROSITA: Dona Catarina's feet are sore with walking, and she can't go any further.

LANDLORD: In that case she must be got to bed.

WIFE: And it's time, too. Long past midnight.

ROSITA: We must hurry, landlord, we must get to Setúbal. The rolling sea is waiting for Dona Catarina.

LANDLORD: The rolling sea will wait till tomorrow. *(To his wife)* This confirms my premonitions. It's a night full of arthritis. *(Loudly, out of the window)* What news of the plague in Lisbon?

ROSITA: The King has died.

LANDLORD: So that's it.

CATARINA: Nonsense, Rosita. Tell him the truth.

LANDLORD: Is that you, Dona Catarina?

CATARINA: Camões died ten years ago of the plague.

LANDLORD: Oh, are you sure?

CATARINA: Quite sure.

ROSITA: Dona Catarina is not accustomed to walking barefoot. For the sake of God's mercy, saddle a donkey for us.

WIFE: Tell them: Not for God's mercy, but for Portuguese ducats. *(To herself)* The King has died. I believe he was a fool. Who would his successor be?

LANDLORD: He was childless.

WIFE: Trust him to be that.

LANDLORD: Just as we are.

WIFE: What about the donkey?

LANDLORD: Hm.

WIFE: Saddle Natercia for them. It will be the ruin of us, but perhaps it will help your arthritis. *(A door opens and shuts.)*

ROSITA *(down below)*: Are you still there, Don Felipe?

WIFE *(calls down)*: He's gone to the stable. Be patient.

136

In the open air.

ROSITA: All will be well, Dona Catarina.

CATARINA: Our religion tells us that. No need for you to repeat it. And in our specific case: all *is* well already.

ROSITA: How so?

CATARINA: The moon is bright enough to show me how you are melting with pity. How foolish! Forgive me for telling you so, Rosita.

ROSITA: Tell me everything.

CATARINA: If only one could! You're always inclined to exaggerate, my child. No, it's much simpler that that: since I've had the plague I've known that the plague exists. And since the plague exists, the other exists no less.

ROSITA: The other?

CATARINA: Don't pretend that you don't understand. You understand much more than you are aware. Didn't you say: I ceased to be afraid of the plague when I found out that it exists.

ROSITA: I did.

CATARINA: Since it's true that Camões died, it's also true that he desired me. His love is the truth, and the plague has given it back to me. What a fine circle it is, worthy of the orbits of the sun and moon. Look at me, Rosita: the plague has given me back my youth. Thanks to the King.

ROSITA: Yes, Dona Catarina.

CATARINA: If it's a good beast, we can be in Setúbal by daybreak. And the rolling sea can be heard some way off.

ROSITA: A long way off.

(The stable door is opened.)

LANDLORD: Get along, Natercia.

ROSITA: No closer, Don Felipe.

LANDLORD: I told you, Dona Catarina, didn't I? I told you the plague was in Lisbon.

CATARINA: Thank you, Don Felipe; thank you.

ROSITA: Come along, Natercia.

LANDLORD: On the left you will find a wineskin, on the right some bread, goat cheese and dates. *(The donkey breaks into a trot.)* I hope you will get home safely.

CATARINA: Thank you, Don Felipe; thank you.

(The donkey's hoof-beats fade.)

from the
DARMSTADT SPEECH
on receiving the
GEORG BÜCHNER PRIZE

...Since the time when the Doctor fed Woyzeck on peas the pretexts have changed. A pure, unbiased, unharnessed Science is now offered to us only with the addendum that its application must, can or — it is hoped — will serve the commonweal. Rose-coloured in this fashion, the soup, Woyzeck's pea soup, which is put in our plates, does taste considerably better. For the eye takes part in the meal, as we were reminded again recently.

We have many new means of allowing ourselves to be kept happy. One of them looks like this: preferably soon after birth, a person's brain is fitted with two tiny electrodes, an installation that does not make undue demands on the surgeon's skill. From this moment, says an American engineer, sense impressions and muscular reflexes can be completely controlled and directed by signals transmitted by special radios under government supervision. Hunger, fear, anger, euphoria, apathy — all of these would be rationed out to us in appropriate doses. No more agony of decision, no more burdensome liberty. Technically, the matter is perfect; all that is needed now is the approval of the administration and the law.

At present it is idle to speculate whether so happy a vision could become reality. What would interest me more is who would be responsible for the radio controls. And without presuming to regard my physical condition as cultural criticism, I confess to cold sweat at the thought of the kind of *élites* that are being called into existence with such convincing arguments. In my mind's eye I see them on team photographs, the beaming participants in courses, all ready to assume their public functions and activate our electrodes. Who will be rejected, who will be chosen, by what standards, and how many Hitlers will be among them?

Power, I am told, is the possibility of forcing human beings to adopt definite behaviour patterns. As our Doctor put it, a most beautifully clear-cut case. But too crude, of course, and too utopian. There are less conspicuous ways of making the world more pleasant, making people happier, power more powerful and its sweetness even sweeter. Ways through the thicket of our mistrust that can be cleared more easily, if our mistrust is an undergrowth that offers serious resistance. If it is more than an indoor plant behind which one fine morning we rub our eyes and

139

wonder who put up the barbed wire and prepared the public burnings.

But barbed wire and public burnings — how crude and inadequate! A cosy sort of inferno. One day — as far as power is concerned — they can safely be dumped and left to rot. There are more subtle instruments now.

It is against one of these more subtle instruments that we propose to take our stand, in the hope of winning the support of that writer in whose name we are gathered here.

A friend of Büchner wrote about him: 'His awareness of the intellectual substance he had gained always impelled him towards a drastic critique of everything that claimed, or succeeded in establishing, an absolute authority in human society or philosophy or art. One could see, by his brow, eyes and lips, that he practised this critique in his secret thoughts even when he was silent.'

The critic Georg Büchner is not known to us as the author of critical essays. True, he studied nature, read historical documents and the records of legal proceedings, but he wrote plays: his form of criticism, secret and silent, a critique translated into imaginative literature, more violent, more bitter and more challenging than any direct attack, because the spectator himself is called upon to judge, to deliver the verdict.

Criticism — a familiar phrase in connection with Büchner, and I assume that I am not alone in regarding it as the key word, the one quality in Büchner that includes every other characterization and attribute: realism, political acumen, grotesqueness, pessimism, irony and even those soap bubbles, the clowning of Valerio and of Prince Leonce, even if at times they are closer to the sky than to our world.

Criticism here means a critical posture, the need, in the face of every object, to probe and inquire before saying yes or no, to ask questions before giving an answer. It will always give offence in those places where an unconditional yes is demanded. In Germany we have only poor specimens of criticism, and even these are little valued. To our ears, in fact, the word itself sounds like an unqualified no. The grim determination with which we recognize authority makes us look upon criticism as a criminal act of defiance or, at best, as a deplorable aberration.

This is the reason too, I think, why Büchner's fame took so long to spread. He is not one of those classics in the family book-case, nor does every sixth-former know his name. There may well be something reassuring about both of these facts, but how did they come about? How did Büchner achieve what was denied to Goethe and Schiller?

Although there was never any doubt as to his poetic distinction, his work clearly aroused an uneasiness, a defence mechanism or, at the very least, an affectionate perplexity — and this in his lifetime as well as in posterity. The perplexity begins with his indubitable date of birth, with the question whether he wasn't born at the wrong time, too late by sixty years. A fine subject for a comedy; but I would say all the same that Heine and Nestroy are a sufficient guarantee of Büchner's contemporaneity. And there is perplexity too in speculations as to how the definitive, lost version of *Woyzeck* may have ended. I quote: 'The biographical records reveal only that the poet did not remain in his nihilistic mood, so that the completed *Woyzeck,* which was written towards the end of his life, may well have been more conciliatory.' And a similar note of gentle regret at the evident failure of Büchner's *Weltanschauung* to attain full maturity strikes me in this account by a friend of Büchner's fiancée, Minna Jaegle: that he thought it both probable and natural that she had exercised a soothing, moderating influence upon him and made him feel more religious. In a current history of literature I read about *Leonce and Lena:* 'A playful nihilism rather than truly comic serenity.'

Minna Jaegle's posthumous papers included nothing in Büchner's hand. Clearly, she destroyed not only letters addressed to her, as she had every right to do, but also other notes and drafts by Büchner, in the fear that they might damage his memory. A younger brother of Büchner's, a Professor of German at a French university who died in 1904, never so much as mentioned his name. Whether the definitive version of *Woyzeck* and Büchner's fourth play, *Pietro Aretino,* were deliberately destroyed, is not known. If unfortunate circumstances were responsible, they were in league with the rest, like the mice whose hunger reduced Büchner's manuscript on the cranial nerves to a fragment.

Against all this, against mice, accident and the loving concern of those near to him, Büchner prevailed. Prevailed not by virtue of the content of his works — there is no such thing as content — but prevailed by virtue of his language. And throughout this address, language understood not quantitatively, as the sum of all the words and grammatical forms used, but qualitatively. By this I do not wish to gain an unfair advantage, to keep open an escape into paradoxes, but to avoid the word style, the style of Goethe's old age, the style of expressionism. What I am after is the quality common to all these styles.

Criticism — and Büchner's art is comprehended in this term — outlives its occasion where language has endowed it with a life of its own. Büchner's contemporaries, the writers of Young Germany, Gutzkow, Mundt, Kühne, Wienbarg — all critically orientated minds as he was — are almost forgotten. Their critical statements may have been urgent and justified, but even about the specific occasions we cannot waste a single word, there is no word left, because nothing they wrote became language. The decisions have been made, the occasions added to the great aggregate. Nothing remains to disturb us, no question mark which language might have preserved for us.

The language of poetry, then, whether informative or not, potentially informative, at any rate, and becoming present, not decorative and certainly more than the conveniences of usage, in which language has its place somewhere between record player and refrigerator, sex and tourism. That other language, then, which like creation itself contains a particle of nothingness, attempting the first topography in an unexplored region. It surprises, startles us, and is incontrovertible; it has the ability to win our agreement, and grows old as soon as that agreement has become general. It is one of our means of acquiring knowledge, *the* means, I am tempted to say. It is precise. To make vagueness one of the essential attributes of the language of poetry is not to denote the merely decorative metaphor, but to attempt to make imaginative literature ineffectual and evade its discomfort. This neutering of language, at once repressive and cunning, is one dominant tendency of its adversary, language control.

What is it in language, though, that is neither neuter nor ineffectual, but uncomfortable and repulsive to language control? First of all, its very existence, the existence of a language that resists control. Next, its ability and its tendency to express itself figuratively. Figures can pose questions or embody questions. But are these the right questions? Are these the questions which lead straight to the answers held in readiness by power? Or could something be called in question by becoming language?

Quite apart from the question-and-answer game of power, the capacity of imaginative literature to provide answers seems slight to me. Even if messages and theses are at stake, their formulation takes place in characters and situations, in compliance with that principle of indirectness which I do not consider outmoded. Besides, why should an author know more about anything than a non-author? The priestly gesture is no longer made, and where the work is cleverer than its author, the reason is most probably that it has run away faster than he has from the answers. The awkward thing about our situation is that the answers arrive before the questions have been put, indeed that many well-disposed people believe in doing away with questions altogether, since there are so many good answers to be had. So one does without them, and the answers flourish and proliferate. They wake us up in the morning, eat wholemeal bread and breathe in the right way, play marches, burn incense and carry red flags or flags of a different colour. No, I am not out for answers; they arouse my mistrust. I opt for the question, for criticism, for the critical poet Georg Büchner, for a type of writer who poses questions and calls things in question. How did Büchner's friend put it? 'Critique of everything that claimed, or succeeded in establishing, an absolute authority.' What is in question is the critique of power, the refusal to say yes to its claims.

My attitude to power, I admit, is rather unreasonable. If power is the indissoluble substance of our world, I am somewhat comforted by the discovery of an anti-substance. When I hear that power has its antecedents even in the animal kingdom, that it is 'a universal phenomenon of social order at every stage of its development and in every sphere of human community and social organization', I reply as follows to people's resentment of my anarchistic instinct: Isn't that to make every exertion of power seem harmless and beyond suspicion? By declaring power to be a universal principle it has been invested with a dubious sort of legitimacy.

And although power was established even before the Fall of Man, I obstinately insist that it is an evil institution. The remark that it will never cease to be active in our world must have been made during a conversation at the hairdresser's.

And I am intensely suspicious of the view that power must be maintained so as to safeguard values. Power has the tendency to become absolute, to become detached from its purpose and establish itself as a value. By maintaining itself, therefore, it can always claim to be maintaining values. Good and evil, in its decisions, are not a matter of choice, but accidents. True enough, power will always point to its ethical foundations when the occasion demands it. But when it does not, power resorts to other methods, the quiet suppression of truth, blatant lies or arguments *ad hoc*. I can think of no kind of inhumanity or depravity, no massacre or terror that was not justified by cunning arguments and presented as good and right. First decapitate your enemies — and rest assured that someone will praise you as a saviour.

143

A concept of the State will be cited, or the struggle for existence, the savagery of nature, or the welfare of the race or the proletariat.

Fine words and fine phrases, but however sweet the coloratura of the sirens' song, on the rocks lie whitening bones for anyone to see. If they lie there long enough, they become part of nature. In the end it becomes a sign of indelicacy to notice them at all.

No, the idea of power does not fill me with ecstasy, I think it abominable, no matter whether power is claimed or established by stealth, won in battle, by violence or by peaceful and lawful means. Might rhymes not only with right, but with night and plight. To me it is the misery and darkness in our lives.

That power harnesses language to its ends is something we should know ever since we had a Ministry or Public Enlightenment and Propaganda. Unfortunately we do not know it. Goebbels, our hard times and our hard hearts, final victory on banners and posters — all this is already historical, it was all over in 1945. Since then language has been no longer bent, pressed, broken and pulverized, language is a means of communication, everyone speaks, writes, reads it freely, anyone can look into it for himself, don't be childish, don't be alarmist, we've more important things to think about. All right, then, I see the point, one shouldn't be suspicious, and language isn't all that important, just a little back passage in our house, and no danger threatens us there. And while we look fixedly into the wide street, where world events are performed for us with conferences and rockets to the moon, a few polite demons have come in and sit at our tables. They start talking, they speak to us, and really it's all very attractive, their sentences make you think — public interests come before private interests — a sentiment you can contradict only if you're an antisocial type. What's disturbing about it is their smile, which invites us to identify ourselves with them. A dangerous augur's smile, what do they mean by it? We open our mouths for a question.

But the answer forestalls it. True, it doesn't quite fit the question we had in mind, but it's very persuasive once again, words and sentences on a high ethical level, and one can't contradict them without descending to a lower level. Even more oppressive than this highly moral tone of theirs is an odour of decay that gradually fills the whole room. We feel like opening the window or at least asking a question.

But there are no longer any questions or windows to be opened. Nothing is in question, everything has been answered, from pregnancy to capital punishment. There are only answers now. They are handed out at a discount, so cheaply that one is forced to think there's no point in asking questions. And that is what they want us to think. Meanwhile they've put bars and railings around the house. They leave us with polite phrases about a good night's rest, and outside a key turns in the lock. We are left to ourselves with a few baskets, crates and sacks full of answers.

As far as answers are concerned, power is generous. Although the text, basically, is always the same, slight variations give an impression of diversity, of open-mindedness and concessions to humanity. Is it not wicked, then, to assert that the general principle behind controlled language is to permit no questions to be asked about questionable things? The answers prove that there are no questionable things. But since we want to be neither augurs nor pure simpletons, we remain suspicious of the answering character of controlled language. Aren't hierarchies of values suggested here, and isn't the rank determined by the interests of power? Are values really at stake, or can they be manipulated to serve those interests? Aren't they interchangeable, and don't they serve to seduce us? And isn't their purpose always to force human beings to adopt a mode of behaviour subservient to power, to train them and make them unanimous?

About controlled language there exists a considerable body of literature which, I fear, is scarcely read, though it could be read. I can therefore refrain from speaking about it, and confine myself to speaking against it. In admitting my polemical intentions let me point out certain words that play a regrettable part in the so-called cultural criticism of our time. Some of them have also been taken up by historians of literature and are often found in passages about Georg Büchner especially. They all assume the character of a final judgement that cannot be contradicted, the character of answers. Disruptive, nihilistic, negative, despairing, intellectual, subversive, impious, etc. As a positive counterpart we are offered the pathos of the golden mean, Western civilization and those cultural values that have crept in unnoticed from the leader columns, reappear as hard work and efficiency and settle down in the finance columns as 'values conducive to industrial prosperity'. That the hierarchy of values presented here as self-evident is determined not by considerations for truth but by exigencies of power could be obvious enough, but it is accepted in our world of faint-hearted conformists without so much as a protest, and

145

one can count on applause if one takes the next step of discrediting anyone who resists power.

The reaction becomes most violent in our country when anyone dares to challenge the most abominable kind of language control, the religious. To say God where one means the devil has become an almost self-evident practice. The word emptied of all meaning in this way remains useful for decorative purposes and helps to embellish the facade. But if anyone pushes aside the paper flowers and reveals the rubbish dump behind them, containing the good, the true, the beautiful, faith, hope and charity, all discarded and covered in filth, if anyone reveals that and asks what is going on, he is destructive, a nihilist and a muck-raker. If one must use the word nihilism, it applies to the processes of power in substituting the empty husks of words for the truth. One cannot speak of God if one does not know what language is. If one does so all the same, one destroys the name and reduces it to a propaganda slogan ...

In language I include the esoteric, experimental, radical kinds. The more drastically it resists language control, the more it conserves true values. It is no accident that power persecutes these kinds of language with uncommon fury. Not because the acceptable content is lacking, but because it is impossible to introduce such a content into it by a conjuring trick. Because something comes into being there that cannot be used by power. It is not content but language that resists power. The partnership of language can prove stronger than the hostility of opinion.

There is a charming, very old aesthetic game, the quarrel about form and content. The golden vessel and the contour that encloses the living body, is how Theodor Storm put it. Gottfried Benn attempted new formulations, and one doesn't need to be much of a prophet to predict eternal life for the problem, right up to the music of the spheres, and it will welcome us on the other planets. It's a problem that cannot be killed, even if we look at it from the point of view of power.

Power suggests that it has solved the problem. Its index finger points in a certain direction: There the mystery lies, and it's no mystery at all, there is only content, everything depends on it, on throne and altar, proletariat, freedom, progress, peace, prosperity, justice, democracy. One feels shamed, one doesn't want to be against everything, and once again we've been tricked by the old magic. We stare at the contents presented to us, and ask no more questions. The problem is solved by the assertion that it doesn't exist or that it doesn't matter.

That is how the stumbling-block of form, of language, is removed. A content that has become language couldn't be removed in this inconspicuous fashion, it would be a great boulder. Power needs a more amenable state of affairs, contents that can be transported and bartered, toy balloons and soap bubbles, a nothing with something wrapped round it. That language control which reduces content to nothing is the means by which content can be put to use. Power rightly senses a certain mercenariness in the inclination to treat every content as genuine currency. That is how inflation begins.

The possession of weapons or of would-be truths, of printing presses, files of documents and ministries — I make the selection easy for myself, I leave nothing out and mean them all, including the past and the present and the future. And I mean not only the German language or any geographical area. Resemblances are growing between the Urals, the Ruhr and Caracas: power, cravings for power, functionaries, key positions. Control over hands and control over souls, both ready to create its vocabulary and syntax.

And yet what we can see of language control may well be only a beginning. Perfection is anticipated in the definition, 'Man is a message.' A definition that fascinates me, though both the fascination and the thing fill me with mistrust. A message from where and to where, or a means of communication over the telegraph wire and the end of all wretched communication and tourism? The definition, whose author is the cyberneticist Norbert Wiener, is not meant as a metaphor and signifies this much at least: We need to devise a practicable language into which the entire man can be translated and so made communicable. This practicable language is being worked out, and the keyword is language as information. Information is still defined as the communication of factual data.

My mistrust is extreme, and I guess that science will one day think realistically, as they put it, and extend its conception of factual data to include what is only potential or desirable: What we are to think, to believe, to hate and to love. The alliance in the East and West alike between reaction and technical progress, the bond between steel helmet and physics, are a likely premiss.

But we are still in the precincts. The roses around us are burgeoning hopefully, and since we are negative, we look for an effective poison that might prevent their flowering. We do not like the possibility of forcing people to adopt predetermined forms of behaviour. Even the

147

prospect of a rise didn't make Woyzeck feel more cheerful. Altogether, we would rather be difficult before we are condemned to silence. It is time for mockery and satire, high time. I for my part suspect that eternal values make power eternal, and our specious delight in things as they are reminds me of the happily obsequious face that I once had to put on. This affirmation of life in controlled language, this perpetual Strength-through-Joy motif and Be Nice to One Another! (But woe betide you if you aren't nice, and woe betide you if you don't rejoice!). Everything getting better, everything positive, our economy, our heroes and our love, why be always looking on the gloomy side, happiness and leisure are on the increase, don't worry about yourselves, we do the worrying for you. This pernicious optimism, so suspect because it is willed and made to measure. Eyes and ears tightly shut and a radiant smile on every face, a song, three and four, that is how we march into the thousand and one kinds of slavery, trusting in the future.

Serious attempts are being made to create the perfectly functioning society. We have no time left to say yes. If our work cannot be understood as criticism, as opposition and resistance, as an awkward question and a challenge to power, then we write in vain, then we are positive and decorate the slaughter-house with geraniums. We should have lost our chance to set down a word in the nothingness of controlled language.

Ladies and gentlemen, by professing a poetry that is opposition, I profess my allegiance to Georg Büchner. At least I assume that such a literature is not wholly uncongenial to his spirit. But in this profession I wish to include a few other allies to whom I assume that Büchner, who wrote *Woyzeck* and *Lenz,* is well disposed. They all belong to the order of the sad demeanour, they are powerless and opposed by instinct to power. And yet, I believe, the dignity of mankind has been entrusted to them. By rebelling and suffering they fulfil our potentialities.

I include all those who refuse to be classified, the lone wolves and outsiders, the heretics in politics and religion, the dissatisfied, the imprudent, the fighters for lost causes, the crackpots, the failures, the unhappy dreamers, the cranks, the spoilsports, all those who cannot forget the misery of the world when they are happy.

POEMS   1955~1972

ZU SPÄT FÜR BESCHEIDENHEIT

Wir hatten das Haus bestellt
und die Fenster verhängt,
hatten Vorräte genug in den Kellern,
Kohlen und Öl,
und zwischen Hautfalten
den Tod in Ampullen verborgen.

Durch den Türspalt sehn wir die Welt:
Einen geköpften Hahn,
der über den Hof rennt.

Er hat unsere Hoffnungen zertreten.
Wir hängen die Bettücher auf die Balkone
und ergeben uns.

TOO LATE FOR MODESTY

We had set the house in order
and curtained the windows,
had provisions enough in the cellars,
coal and oil,
and between wrinkles had hidden
death in medicine bottles.

Through a chink in the door we see the world:
A beheaded cock
running across the yard.

He has trampled our hopes.
We hang up our sheets on the balconies
and give in.

BESTELLUNG

Fünf Gänge,
sag es den hölzernen Mädchen,
für den Pfennig unter der Zunge,
und die Teller gewärmt.

Ihr habt uns hingehalten
mit Fasanen und Stör,
Burgunder und Bouillabaisse.
Tragt endlich die Speise auf,
die es nicht gibt,
und entkorkt die Wunder!

Dann wollen wir gern
die Mäuler öffnen
und was wir schuldig sind
zahlen.

ORDER

Five courses,
tell them, the wooden girls,
for the penny beneath the tongue,
and the plates warmed up.

You tried to keep us happy
with pheasant and sturgeon,
champagne and bouillabaisse.
Enough of that. Now serve
the dish that doesn't exist
and uncork the miracles.

Gladly then
we'll open our gobs
and pay
the bill that's due.

SCHIFFAHRT DER GÄRTEN

Ausruhend auf einem Ast
verlernte die Amsel das Fliegen:
Eine Bö in die Takelage
von Tannen und Lichtmasten,
eine Rose irrtümlich,
als die Schlüssel klirrten.

Die Amselaugen
erraten, wer öffnen wird:
Eiserne Treppen aufwärts
auf ein grasiges Deck,
Stimmen gehen genug
durch die Korridore.

GARDENS AFLOAT

Resting on a bough
the blackbird forgot how to fly.
A gust in the rigging
of pines and lamp masts,
a rose by mistake
when the keys clinked.

Those blackbird eyes
guess who will open:
Iron steps going up
to a grassy deck,
voices enough
pass through the corridors.

FUSSNOTE ZU ROM

Ich werfe keine Münzen in den Brunnen,
ich will nicht wiederkommen.

Zuviel Abendland,
verdächtig.

Zuviel Welt ausgespart.
Keine Möglichkeit
für Steingärten.

FOOTNOTE TO ROME

I'll drop no coin into the fountain,
I have no wish to return.

Too Western by half,
Suspect.

Too much of the world left out.
No provision
for gardens of sand and rock.

ZUM BEISPIEL

Zum Beispiel Segeltuch.

Ein Wort in ein Wort übersetzen,
das Salz und Teer einschließt
und aus Leinen ist,
Geruch enthält,
Gelächter und letzten Atem,
rot und weiß und orange,
Zeitkontrollen
und den göttlichen Dulder.

Segeltuch und keins,
die Frage
nach einer Enzyklopädie
und eine Interjektion
als Antwort.

Zwischen Schöneberg
und Sternbedeckung
der mystische Ort
und Stein der Weisen.

Aufgabe, gestellt
für die Zeit nach dem Tode.

FOR INSTANCE

For instance sailcloth.

Translate a word into a word
that includes salt and tar
and is made of linen,
contains a smell,
laughter and dying breath,
red and white and orange,
time study
and the divine sufferer.

Sailcloth and none,
the question
about an encyclopaedia
and for answer
an interjection.

Between Scarborough
and stellar occultation
the mystical locus
and philosopher's stone.

A task, set
for the time after death.

TIMETABLE

Diese Flugzeuge
zwischen Boston und Düsseldorf.
Entscheidungen aussprechen
ist Sache der Nilpferde.
Ich ziehe vor,
Salatblätter auf ein
Sandwich zu legen und
unrecht zu behalten.

TIMETABLE

Those aeroplanes
between Boston and Düsseldorf.
It's up to hippopotamuses
to pronounce decisions.
I prefer
to lay lettuce leaves
on a sandwich and
remain in the wrong.

VERSPÄTUNG

Da bin ich gewesen
und da,
hätte auch
dorthin fahren können
oder zuhaus bleiben.

Ohne aus dem Hause zu gehen,
kannst du die Welt erkennen.
Laotse begegnete mir
früher als Marx.
Aber eine
gesellschaftliche Hieroglyphe
erreichte mich im linken Augenblick,
der rechte war schon vorbei.

TOO LATE

I have been there
and there,
could have travelled to
that place as well
or stayed at home.

Without leaving the house
you can know the world.
Laotzu came my way
earlier than Marx.
But a
social hieroglyph
reached me at the left moment,
the right had already passed.

LANGE GEDICHTE

NORMAL

Sagt ihm,
er soll die Gabel links nehmen
und das Messer rechts.
Einarmig gilt nicht.

VORSICHT

Die Kastanien blühn.
Ich nehme es zur Kenntnis,
äußere mich aber nicht dazu.

ZUVERSICHT

In Saloniki
weiß ich einen, der mich liest,
und in Bad Nauheim.
Das sind schon zwei.

STILLE POST FÜR JEDES JAHR

Ich sag dir den ersten Januar ins Ohr.
Sag ihn weiter, ich warte.

ZWISCHENBESCHEID FÜR BEDAUERNSWERTE BÄUME

Akazien sind ohne Zeitbezug.
Akazien sind soziologisch unerheblich.
Akazien sind keine Akazien.

LONG POEMS

NORMAL

Tell him
to hold the fork with his left hand,
the knife with his right.
One-armed does not count.

CAUTION

The chestnuts are flowering.
I take note of that
but do not remark on it.

CONFIDENCE

In Saloniki
I know of one man who reads me,
and in Bad Nauheim.
That makes two already.

SILENT POST FOR EVERY YEAR

I whisper January the first into your ear.
Pass it on, I shall wait.

INTERIM REPORT FOR PITIABLE TREES

Acacias are deficient in topical relevance.
Acacias are sociologically unimportant.
Acacias are not acacias.

PAPIERZEIT

Urkunden und Aquarelle
bewahrt der Erzvater
in Papprollen auf.
Künftigen Forschern ein Zufall,
ist es doch weise Voraussicht.

BEITRAG ZUM DANTEJAHR

Chandler ist tot
und Dashiell Hammett.
Mir liegts nicht,
mich an das Böse schlechthin
zu halten und
Dante zu lesen.

ODE AN DIE NATUR

Wir haben unsern Verdacht
gegen Forelle, Winter
und Fallgeschwindigkeit.

HART CRANE

Mich überzeugen
die dünnen Schuhe, der
einfache Schritt über Stipendien
und Reling hinaus.

PAPER TIME

The patriarch preserves
records and water colours
in cardboard rolls.
For future researchers a windfall,
it's a wise provision too.

CONTRIBUTION TO THE DANTE YEAR

Chandler is dead
and so is Dashiell Hammet.
It's not in my nature
to take evil
neat and
read Dante.

ODE TO NATURE

We have our suspicions
against trouts, winter
and the speed of falling bodies.

HART CRANE

What convinces me
is the shoes, the
simple step beyond writers' grants
and the boat's rail.

SPÄTER

Erfahrungen abdrehen
und ungehemmt
zählen bis
93, auch weiter.

Jedenfalls
für die Silvesternacht
1999
bin ich verabredet.
Weiter im Gebirge, auf
einem Kanapee,
freue mich, man hat
wenig Abwechslung.

LATER

Turn off experiences
and without inhibition
count up to
93, or farther.

Anyway,
for New Year's Eve
1999
I have a date.
Farther up the mountains, on
a couch,
I'm pleased, one has
so few diversions.

NOMADEN

Zeit für mich,
das Gebirge abzukarren.
Ich hätte das Land gern flach.

Ich dachte:
Plattdeutsche Sätze,
Nomaden,
die an ihren teppichfreien
Tagen kommen, um mich
herumgehen und flüstern
aus dem Koran, plattdeutsch.

Wer kommt, hat sich
in meine Irrtümer verlaufen,
geht ohne Anruf davon.

NOMADS

Time for me
to cart away the mountains.
I'd like the land to be flat.

I thought:
sentences in Low German,
nomads
who come on their
carpet-free days, walk
around me and whisper
from the Koran, in Low German.

Those who come
have lost their way in my errors,
leave without being addressed.

VERLÄSSLICHER KRITIKER

Das Wichtige
läßt er aus.
So weiß man immer,
was wichtig ist.

Er bespricht
Fürze von gestern
und Fürze von heute.
Sein Entdeckerglück:
Ein Furz von morgen.

RELIABLE CRITIC

He always leaves out
the essential thing.
That way one can always tell
what it is.

He reviews
yesterday's farts
and today's.
The discovery that delights him is
one of tomorrow's farts.

HART CRANE

Ausgezogene Schuhe. Ein Stilleben von
kaputten Birnen, jetzt
fallen wir, kein
Lachen, keine
Barockmusik hält uns auf,
jetzt
die Lampen, die Schuhe,
wir, wie konnten
Umarmungen uns halten,
die Kälte ist wahr, wir
und
die Schuhe.

HART CRANE

Shoes taken off. A still life of
blown bulbs, now
we fall, no
baroque music detains us,
now
light bulbs, the shoes,
as for us, how could
embraces hold us,
what's true is the cold, ourselves
and
the shoes.

LANGE GEDICHTE

Zugetan den
Hühneraugenoperateuren,
heimlich saufenden
Nachtschwestern,
Leichenwäschern, Abortfrauen.

Abgeneigt
prominenten Friseuren,
Fürstenhochzeiten,
Brechtplatten,
realistischer Literatur

LONG POEMS

Well disposed towards
operators on corns,
night nurses who drink
on the quiet,
washers of corpses, lavatory attendants.

Inimical
to prominent hairdressers,
royal weddings,
Brecht recordings,
realistic literature.

EN ATTENDANT

Am Dienstag stellten wir noch
die Abfälle vors Haus,
am Mittwoch
boten wir das Haus an,
am Donnerstag uns,
aber die Müllabfuhr
ließ uns aus.
So bleiben wir und hoffen
auf bessere Wochen und
die Bestechlichkeit der Träger.

EN ATTENDANT

On Tuesday we still
put our garbage in front of the door,
on Wednesday
we put the house on the market,
on Thursday ourselves,
but the refuse collectors
missed us out.
So we stay and hope
for better weeks and
dustmen who can be bribed.

VOM GLÜCK

Vom Glück
bleiben zwei Papageien übrig,
der Münzfernsprecher.
Die Sätze wird jemand fortsetzen,
der recht hat
und die passenden Münzen.
Mich verläßt mein Gedächtnis,
ich vergesse den eigenen Namen.
Das Grau des Papageiengefieders
ist schwer zu benennen.

OF HAPPINESS

Of happiness
two parrots remain,
the coin-fed telephone.
My sentences will be completed
by someone who's right
and has the coins that fit.
My memory leaves me,
I forget my own name.
The grey of the parrot's plumage
is hard to denote.

ÄPFEL

Äpfel kann man in Holz schnitzen
und als Kreisel drehn.
Sie sagen etwas
in einer Sprache, die
keiner mehr spricht,
ich weiß noch Vokabeln davon,
habe auch ein Wörterbuch
aber nach einiger Zeit
hört mir niemand mehr zu
ich habe
einen flüsternden Bariton,
der erbittert.

APPLES

Apples can be carved out of wood
and spun as tops.
They say something
in a language that
no one speaks any more,
I still know snatches of it,
have a dictionary too
but after a while
no one listens to me.
I have
a whispering baritone voice
that embitters.

MOLES
PROSE POEMS
1966~1972

HOUSEMATES

Nothing in the world is more repugnant to me than my parents. Wherever I go they pursue me. No removal, no foreign travel helps. As soon as I've found a chair the door opens and one of the two stares in, Father State or Mother Nature. I throw a pen, all in vain. They get into a huddle, they understand each other. In the kitchen Household sits, pale, skinny and intimidated. He's pretty revolting too, I sometimes feel sorry for him. He's no relation of mine, but not to be got rid of.

For half an hour literature gives me pleasure. The Kinks, I reflect, are so much better than the Dave Clark Five. But suddenly she's back, her mouth smeared with blood, and shows me her latest model. Everything split in two, she says, a stylistic principle, male and female. Can't you think of anything better, I ask. Come off it, old boy, she says. Here's the praying mantis. While his rear mates with her she devours his front. Pooh, I say, Mum, you're unappetizing. But think of sunsets, she titters.

I try to calm down and try to add a few lines to my biography of Bakunin. That Marx did for you once and for all, Michael Alexandrovitch, I say out loud, and Dad's there in my room. He's fiddling about with a recruit's bone. Under his suspicious gaze I cover my manuscript with the National News. You give too few readings, he says, and not till he's left do I notice that he's taken my wallet.

In the kitchen Household sits weeping uninhibitedly. I close my eyes and stick my fingers into my ears. Rightly so.

EPISODE

I wake up and find myself in a state of emergency, I'm not sure why, but take the precaution of arresting my children. Arrests are indispensable. On the radio I pick out rock, turn the aerial in the direction of Luxembourg. Clanking my handcuffs I patrol the floors. On the first floor all is normal, and in the cellar too, but elsewhere? There's no telling, no seriousness, nothing to depend on banana skins on the stairs. That's where you end up if you don't keep a tight hold on the reins.

Under the roof complete anarchy reigns, someone is reading Leroi Jones, my landlady's asleep, at eighty she ought to know what's to be done. Webern is on the turntable, that's how dissolute it is, and the walls are full of mould. Counter-measures. Order is half of life, and the other half too. With moist eyes I hear the news from Headquarters. They're congratulating themselves, everything is taking a turn for the better, the penal laws are already amended and waiting in drawers. On the second floor they're coming to terms with the new state of affairs, beginning to think realistically. A policeman from Berlin, on leave, takes charge of martial law and the fire extinguishers. No lack of idealism.

By eleven I have the ground floor under control, with the help of some reinforcements, but not many. By twelve I'm sorting out seditious and corrupting literature. At one I summon the tenants for a briefing in the form of a luncheon. At two policemen surrounded the house and arrest the lot of us.

Everything has been quiet ever since.

IECUR

Iecur, the liver, a word that's all the rage in Lithuanian, from Albania too one can learn things one will never get out of one's head again, much as one would like to.

Iecur, the liver, that's easy to take with you on short and longer journeys, angry assistant professors hasten to concur and take their seats beside the driver, without worrying about the traffic. Celtologists and Iranists can be tripped up under the same head, covered with a straw hat that can be worn in rainy weather — they even recommend it for monsoons. Most people don't think of that.

Iecur, the liver, an Indo-Germanic delicacy that drives onions into one's eyes. I know all about that, I sat in Lecture Room 13, large enough for at least twenty lady linguists, and sat there alone. From time to time a Slavist, expert in the wine bars of Belgrade.

Iecur, the liver, Sartre must have other words in mind, it's rare in Dante, quite absent in Wittgenstein. Only Prometheus, but of him only a scream is extant, and that's hard to classify.

HOMAGE TO BAKUNIN

Five of us have gathered, inconspicuously shaved. We've succeeded in re-acquiring the burial ground and we're celebrating that with a small womanless service. Since revolutionaries in transit have got into the habit of laying down spent cartridge cases as a tribute — even rusted daggers have been found in the ivy — we're now trying to subvert the tourist advertisers and are planning our own anarchistic brochures.

A.B. and B.C. are amongst us. The service is a silent one. We are meditating on our revered precursor, and on other things too. I, for instance, on the first day of the month. How often he himself may have meditated on that! Later, over a gloomy beer, we intend to compare meditations, which will bring out our old division into friends and opponents of Marx. At the moment the score is 3–2, but it isn't even half-time. Cement governments and concrete states are gaining ground.

Meditations on wax flowers and on the level of clay jars. Autumn leaves are too natural, Saigon is too topical. It suits us to be a hundred years behind or a hundred years in advance. We believe in the sciences and in utopia, meditate only at gravesides, otherwise we keep active. We omit resolutions, celebrate fools and their hopeless last stands.

But who will have thought of Bakunin? Not even I, not of his prisons, not of his Siberia, not of his abandoned Locarno. I hope he spent a few pleasant and sunny days there at least, and that they warmed his beard.

LINES TO HUCHEL

For April 3rd I have no agenda but hooded crows, shrikes and paraffin from the store. That's quite enough, my memory is feeble, I have to jot down those things or form a word like Neneupe, it sounds like a Muse, sounds Greek. If I had other projects the result would be an Aztec deity, that's how stupid my memory is, ethnography whirrs around in it with clipped auxiliary wings.

It would be better if red-bellied toads were on my agenda, but that's how it fell out. Red-bellied toads are a leitmotiv, they ring, paraffin is fortuitous. The reason is that I don't put any order into my future, everything flies into my morning drunkenness, I gobble it up, am not silicitous, as I used to be. I don't know how it is with you. Now I even eat spinach, though preferably not minced.

A prolonged winter, it's always like that here, a prolonged consumption of ice. The shrikes are not nesting yet, in avalanches from the roof, tiles come crashing down in front of the house, I'm collecting for a new one, but shan't get far enough, everything is too obvious. Otherwise there's nothing new, only dates of the day, month and year. I think that the snow will stay.

I know only a few words of Irish, but must make do with them in Ireland because I speak no English. I have the same trouble with Welsh in Wales and with Gaelic in Scotland. I say 'Loch Ness', and at once I'm a linguistic prodigy and a noted Celtologist.

It's harder in England, but there my subterfuge is to Esperanto as I wander from conurbation to conurbation. Esperanto is easy, boyo the boy, everyone understands that. It isn't quite as easy as English, but almost.

I'd have no difficulty at all in Greece, there I understand everything, ancient Greek, modern Greek, Greek Orthodox. Nowhere is Greek as widely diffused as in Greece. This fact is usually not given the attention it deserves. How noteworthy it is would be worthily noted if the country were called not Greece but China. This only as an instance of what is astonishing about the little things around us.

Now back to Ireland.